feasts of unrule

feasts
of
unrule

Feasts of Unrule is a condensed treatise on the philosophy of right & on human rights in general, & on the genealogy of morals in particular. In dialogue with Arendt & Derrida, Armand critiques the ascendency of Platonic "reason" to the detriment of poetry (so-called unreason), humanity, freedom & the liberty of one's own soul. Against Sartre, Armand argues that for a free-spirited poetry "to choose truth" is to be "committed" to writing, itself. In the present revenance of Cold War apocalypticism, such poetry is suppressed wherever it disputes a social order that desires to "own" the rhetoric of terror. Through the dissident writings of Darwish, Goytisolo & Rimbaud, **Feasts of Unrule** challenges the compulsive doublespeak of those regimes of "impossibility" – from Russia & Israel to the invisible third eye of capital – that stand in the way of a decolonization of western mind. Louis Armand's latest book is a poetic outcry & a howl against the dogmas of corporate-state power. *Nina Živančević*

Louis Armand has long & systematically explored the transformations of literature, literary theory & literary culture in an era in which information technology & digitization have penetrated all these fields. His new book of essays, **Feasts of Unrule,** provides compelling testimony that, within the framework of conventional language, literary discourse is always potentially subversive, insofar as it is able to break out of a subservient relation to power & become a spectre that haunts it. Armand doesn't agitate for an "enagaged literature" in the Sartrean sense, but for a literature that engages with resistance, even at the cost of being accused of disrespect for reason, humanism & other vices. *Miroslav Petříček*

FEASTS OF UNRULE

LOUIS ARMAND

Introduced by Manuel João Neto

litteraria pragensia books
CCCT, Filozofická Fakulta, Univerzita Karlova
Náměstí Palacha 2, 116 38 Praha 1, Czech Republic
www.litterariapragensia.com

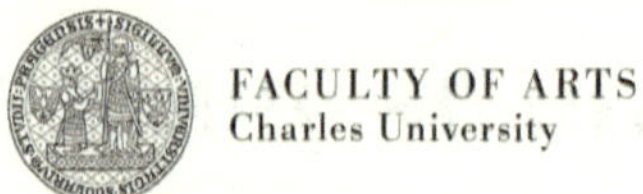

ISBN 978-80-7671-149-5
1st edition, 2024

The four numbered sections of this volume comprised *Festins de Desmando*, trans. Jorge Pereirinha Pires (Lisbon: Barco Bêbedo, 2023). "Avant-Trans" was presented at the European Neo-Avant-Garde Network conference, "Translation as Creation," Université de Liège, 31 November 2023. A version of "Incipit Parodia" was presented under the title "Combative Literary Theory & a Theory of the State" as a keynote lecture at the Laboratory of Comparative Humanities conference, "Comparative Studies: Issues in Theory, Criticism & Pedagogy," Ibn Zor University, Agadir, 9 February 2023 & published in *NON* (21 November 2023). "Literature | Theory | Ideology" was published in *Critique, théorie littéraire et idéologie*, eds. Jean Bessière & Dorothy Figueira (Paris: Honoré Champion, 2024). "Crisis in the Time Machine" was presented at the 8th European Network for Avant-Garde & Modernism Studies conference, "Globalising the Avant-Garde," NOVA FCSH, Lisbon, 1 September 2022 & was published in *Minor Literature[s]* (March 2024). "Object Situations [from the Surrealist Situation of the Object to the Lacanian *objet a*]," was presented at the Centre for European Modernism Studies conference, "The Materiality of Modernisms," Colégio Almada Negreiros, NOVA FCSH, Lisbon, 16 December 2022 & published in *The Materiality of Modernisms*, eds. Giorgia Casara *et al.* (Milan: Ledizione, 2024). A version of "All Things New" was published as "Languages of the Unspeakable" in *ALIENIST* (October 2023). "Soft Targets" was published in *Overland* (March 2024). The introduction by Manuel João Neto was originally published, in Portuguese, in *A Batalha* (January 2024).

The author wishes to extend their thanks to David Vichnar, Michel Delville, Emanuel Cameira, Mariana Gomez, El Habib Louai, Jean Bessière, Nina Živančević, Miroslav Petříček, Philipp Teuchmann, Siegmar Fricke, Jonathan Dunk, Giorgia Casara & Manuel João Neto.

Research for this work was supported by the European Regional Development Fund-Project "Creativity & Adaptability as Conditions of the Success of Europe in an Interrelated World" (No. CZ.02.1.01/0.0/0.0/16_019/0000734).

What is rational is actual;
& what is actual is rational.
(Hegel, "Preface" to *The Philosophy of Right*)

THE TEXT IS [NOT] A VOID INTO WHICH MEANING FALLS

Louis Armand is an essayist fluent in the marginality of literature & this collection of essays, gathered under the designation *Festins de Desmando*, approaches a psychoanalytic (or metatextual, to be more precise) inquiry into the sense that marginality assumes in the current literary context.

In Armand's analytical framework, an eminently Marxist nature is intuited, as he assumes the opposition between two distinct languages (literature & power), & from this theoretical framework he discusses how "aberrant textual bodies" can be incorporated into the symbolic systems of politics. According to the author, the gears of this dialectic are activated by two reflex movements: on the one hand, the rupture that literary fictions occasionally inflict on the ideological systems of politics &, on the other hand, the attempt of power to neutralize the vanguard operating in the margins as an "object of (potential) rhetorical capture." In this history of "discontinuities" – in contrast to a history of nexuses – the monster we call collective reason is engendered, unifying two antagonistic modes of representation: literature & politics, art & life.

If in this framework Armand's theory bears fruit from various perceptive angles that deserve to be considered & discussed. It is, however, in the exploration of the intrinsic insufficiencies of the Hegelian epistemological scheme that the most interesting paths offered by this collection of essays are cleared. In other words, by breaking with the initial schematism, the author questions how we can answer the question of the meaning that the marginal assumes when we reverse the terms of the initial premise, moving from the perspective of literature as power to that of power as literature – especially since the latter sometimes takes the form of (using the interesting designation used by the author) a *doppelganger* of ideology. In essence, with this inversion, we formulate the following question: "Is not all political discourse a plot invented by literature itself?"

By adding this third interstitial text, contiguous to both power & literature, but identifying exclusively with neither, Armand progressively moves away from the Marxist paradigm & progressively approaches an interpretation of the spectral forms of discourse, more fluid & interpenetrable than materialistic forms. Because politics is the rhetorical art of the possible & writing the enunciation of an impossibility, both are found, despite being fundamentally antagonistic, in their ambition to become-worldview – or, in Armand's words, in the form of "myths animated by failure" exposing the intrinsic entropy of the systems we navigate.

According to the formulation that the philosopher Boris Groys has employed in his most recent texts, the literary or artistic work is always a call from the future addressed to an absent recipient – an idea that, curiously, resonates in these *Feasts of Unrule*. The logical conclusion will be that revolution also seems to first enunciate itself in the form of myth (or literature) to later, in the hypothetical future, inscribe itself in the fabric of reality as a *de facto* regime. Both discourses placed in opposition (marginal literature & revolutionary ideology) end up converging, therefore, in an unusual extremity where past meanings fall, to be re-elaborated into meanings projected in the time to come, as forms of madness inoculated in reason.

Manuel João Neto

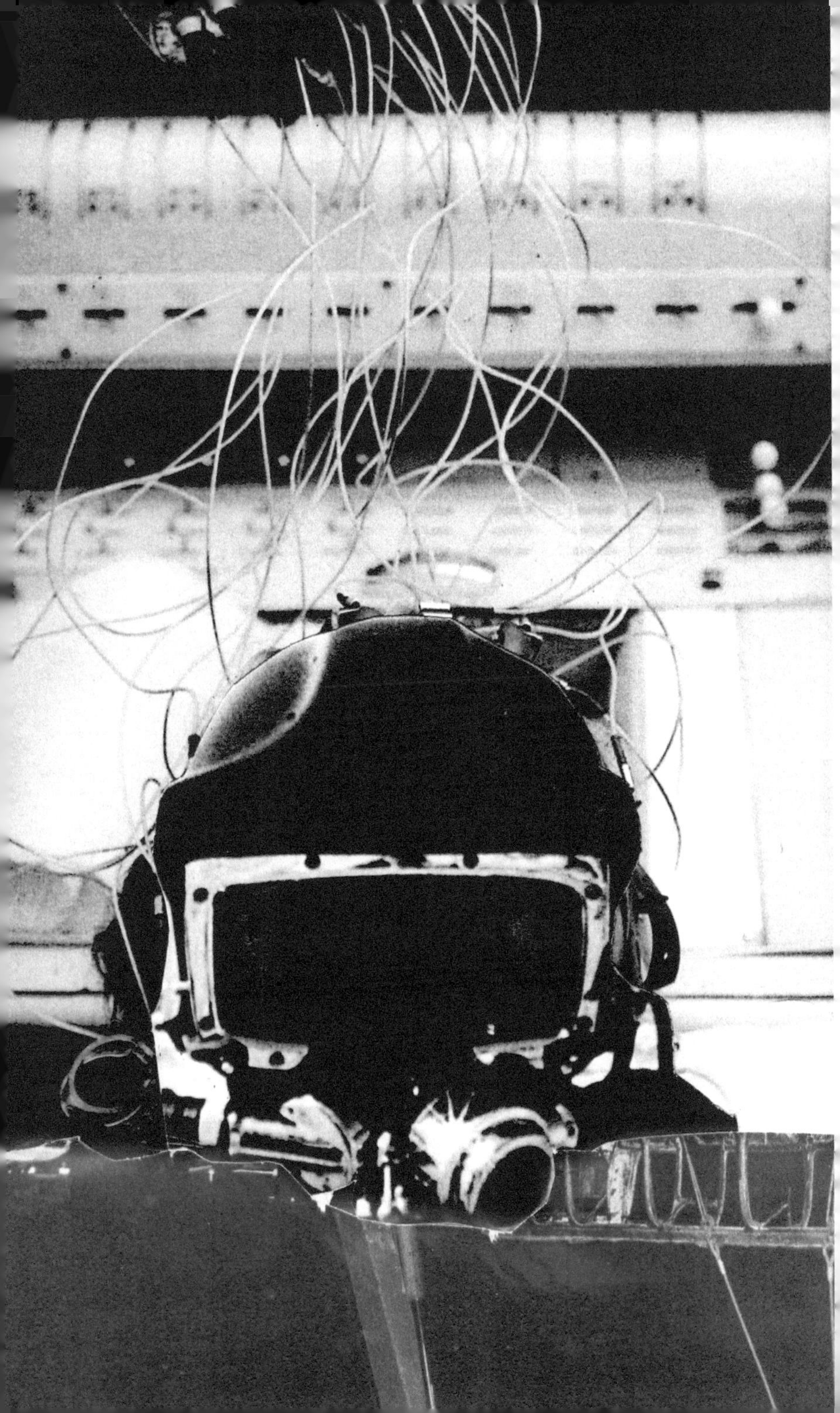

SOFT TARGETS

...the fearsome, word-&-thought-defying banality of evil.
(Hannah Arendt, *Eichmann in Jerusalem*)

There is, in the minds of those whose very being is calibrated to that proverbial Doomsday Clock, an eternal recurrence wherein, like protagonists in a science fiction fantasy, they are constantly reliving the unfinished business of the Cold War: an eternally recurring glitch in time, where it will always be 90 seconds to midnight & history will always be just about to end. It's necessary to grasp that, from this unique vantage, both the war in Ukraine & the putative genocide in Gaza can only be viewed as the decisive "struggle" – the one that Cold War doctrine denied its protagonists the gratification of submitting to an ultimate proof. In this parallel universe, the Doomsday Clock may yet strike the hour, not with a dialectical whimper but with all the apocalyptic *jouissance* of a "final solution" whose contemporary avatars see themselves as archangels at the Last Judgement. To these minds, the imprisoning fantasy of a "liberal democratic world order" can indeed be brought to a happy end & the chosen ones be permitted, at long last, to march triumphant into the nuclear sunset – or at least to raise their flags over the desolation of Bakhmut, Avdiivka & Rafah, if nothing else.

Bringing the war back home

On 21 December 2023, at 14:59, a terrorist armed w/ a ZEV AR15 military assault rifle opened fire in the upper corridors of the Philosophy Faculty at Charles University, Prague, killing 14 & wounding 25. Students & colleagues – attending lectures, taking end-of-year exams & preparing an afternoon programme of Christmas carols. Bodies lay on the floor. One survivor sustained seven bullet wounds.[1] Hundreds had to be evacuated while the terrorist continued to fire from the rooftop into the street. In the rightwing media this became a story about yet another misunderstood whiteboy, suicided by those institutions of liberal "woke" propaganda otherwise known as the humanities.[2] Throughout, the socalled mainstream media persisted in referring to this terrorist by the asinine term "shooter," as if the corridors of the Philosophy Faculty were simply a target range with cardboard silhouettes. And by a perverse role-reversal, one seen too often before, the victims almost immediately became the "culprits," accused of responsibility for the very terror inflicted upon them & targeted by hate speech that filtered even into the nation's parliament. While such actions are easily dismissed as belonging to "fringe elements," they in fact represent a far more general & persistent totalitarianism operating just below the threshold of the State (the neofascist SPD,[3] one of whose deputies openly defamed the victims under parliamentary privilege, is the fastest growing political movement in the Czech Republic & holds 20 seats in the legislature). Nor is the language of intolerance & victim-shaming merely "a primal shelter to compensate for personal disarray,"[4] making perverse demands upon our sympathy for these hapless mouthpieces of reactionary ideology; it is nothing short of a *motive force of social capture* – which is to say *coup d'état* – ruthlessly operating by means of "culture war."

It was the view held by Hannah Arendt that wherever "civic life has become a vacuum or a farce, the forces of cultural barbarism

---

[1] See https://english.radio.cz/novinky-one-25-people-injured-prague-shooting-remains-critical-condition-8804805

[2] The murderer "evaded justice" by shooting himself in the head.

[3] Svoboda a přímá demokracie [Freedom & Direct Democracy].

[4] Julia Kristeva, "What of Tomorrow's Nation"? *Nations Without Nationalism*, trans. Leon A. Roudiez (New York: Columbia University Press, 1993) 2.

can be counted on to fill the void."[5] Such forces can't be dismissed as opportunistic hyenas coming out of the wilderness into the precincts of "civilisation" to thieve from upturned rubbish bins; they are themselves the *agents of farce* & the very *architects of this void*. As Arendt must have known, on 17 November 1939 these same forces of barbarism stormed the Philosophy Faculty & other university buildings in Prague, arrested & later shot 9 professors & students involved in organising protests against the Nazi occupation, & deported 1,200 more to Sachsenhausen & other deathcamps.[6] 17 November, subsequently commemorated as International Students Day, was also the date in 1989 on which student protests against the Soviet puppet regime in Prague initiated the socalled Velvet Revolution. For many years "17. listopadu" has been the name of the street adjoining the Philosophy Faculty on Jan Palach Square, the latter memorialising a student of history & political economy who, on 16 January 1969, set himself alight in protest against the Warsaw Pact invasion which had terminated the period of social reform known as the Prague Spring, dying three days later. The site of the 21 December terror attack is no mere "ivory tower," then. It emerges from the 20th century rather as a kind of dissident institution within civil society itself — one in which a critical consciousness of the "philosophy of state" & its totalising apparatuses has somehow managed to persist *despite its institutional status* & in spite of every effort at normalisation both from within its own bureaucracy & by those external regimes of power to which its mere existence is anathema.

Who owns the rhetoric of terror?
Through the prism of the long 20th century, we have reached the inverse of that sentiment famously expressed in the first of Rilke's *Duino Elegies*: "For *beauty* is nothing / but the *beginning of terror*, which we can still barely endure, / & while we stand in wonder it coolly disdains / to destroy us."

In the immediate aftermath of 21 December, news outlets repeatedly cited "security officials" to the effect that, by not being the work of a member of a designated terrorist organisation, the

[5] Hannah Arendt, *The Human Condition* (Chicago: University of Chicago Press, 1958) 6.
[6] The university remained closed for the duration of the war.

attack on the Philosophy Faculty[7] could not be deemed a "terrorist attack." *Terror*, like *tragedy*, is a bespoke term. As are *war* & *genocide*. In these, the language of the "individual" is partitioned from that of the "state," just as that of "aesthetics" is partitioned from that of "politics." Economies of linguistic power circulate within a system that is self-authorising, self-perpetuating, & from which the poetics of everyday life is ostensibly alienated (beyond the spasms of satirical critique). Jacques Derrida alludes to this system under the neologism *economimesis.*[8] That is to say, as an economy of representation wherein the valorisation of *what* is represented & *how* it is represented is bound to a profit mechanism, a systemic bias that *capitalises on itself.* The "Prague Shootings," as the events of 21 December have since been dubbed, are no exception: the tension between survivor narratives & official discourse (21.12 as a "national tragedy") is obvious, & this dissonance has been especially visible in a media driven by reflexive sensationalism.

For Arendt, such an *economimesis* is at work in producing the media cult of "individual life" & its analogue in the "life of the species" which, as Julia Kristeva remarks, "tries to impose itself as the supreme modern good."[9] It is *in their name* that the rhetoric of terror is evoked & maintained. Arendt alludes to this signifying regime as a "single-minded activism" in which the political has been elided with a Kantian categorical imperative (a pseudo-ethics). One vector of this thought is Sartre's existentialist phenomenology, which produces a "paranoid subject" (Roquentin & his epiphany of the pebble-on-the-beach) whose ethic of being-for-the-world by individual, committed action merely inverts the paranoiac's belief in a conspiratorial world operating exclusively upon *it*. Sartre's committed individual is the paranoiac's sublimation of the experience of being inscribed within the gaze-of-the-other (that is to say, under the sway of a transcendental signified: pure reason or the state). The irony for Arendt is that "the pervasiveness of an egocentric... attitude toward public life" contributes to making

---

[7] This synecdoche, between individual victims & institution, prefigures the discussion below of Hajjaj's "I am not a number & I do not consent to my death being passing news."

[8] Jacques Derrida, "Economimesis," trans. R. Klein, *Diacritics* 11.2 (1981): 2-25.

[9] Julia Kristeva, *Hannah Arendt: Life Is a Narrative*, trans. Frank Collins (Toronto: University of Toronto Press, 2001) 7.

"totalitarianism possible."[10] It is the tragedy of western civilisation that totalitarianism is itself *immanent* to liberal democracy's self-image (media): a selfoimage through which "the political sphere" comes to be seen "as merely the administrative & protective apparatus required by the *economic* realm... Increasingly, the economic sphere subsumes all others."[11] As in Derrida's *economimesis*, the paranoid subject mirrors a totalising economic system of meaning's production-consumption.

If poetry's supposed alienation from the world is a metaphor for the work of alienation *in general* across the sphere of everyday life – of an apparent acquiescence to economic totalitarianism (& its ungainly remainder) – then the question arises as to what stands beyond the "impossibility" ascribed to this system of totalisation? What mode of critique or *détournement* corresponds to this system's *insufficiency* (for, a system of totalisation can only operate on the proviso that it *doesn't* totalise; instead it produces an *image of totality*, to which it pretends the whole of reality corresponds). Were we to name this ungainly remainder, this insufficiency, *poetry* – as Arendt suggests – then in a situation where *realpolitik* (as *total representation*) can be affected only through radical "poetic" praxis, the concern with language demands priority.

War on terror

While it is easy to reject as fake political processes & referenda staged in overtly manipulated media environments like Hong Kong & Russian-occupied Ukraine,[12] it remains a virtual taboo (conspiranoia) to critique the relation of privately owned media conglomerates to the subversion of democratic processes in western liberal democracies. This has been tested in recent times by referenda in the UK & Australia (Brexit; the Indigenous Voice to Parliament) in which manipulation of public discourse has not only been comparable to the fraudulence visible in the former Soviet sphere (& in pseudo-democratic colonies of authoritarian regimes,

---

[10] Arendt, *The Human Condition*, 6.
[11] Arendt, *The Human Condition*, 5.
[12] Mindful of the fact, here, that the Kremlin's "justification" for its full-scale invasion of Ukraine on 24 February 2022 hinged on two points: protecting ethnic Russians against *genocide*; & *denazification*.

such as Hong Kong), but is nakedly so. The representation of "terror" in the western media has long been a measure of its much-vaunted press independence. The Global *War on Terror* (GWOT), launched by the United States in the wake of the World Trade Centre attacks on 11 September 2001, can be considered the apogee of an historical movement to annex this term. In this respect "terror" stands as a counterpart to the legitimate usage of the term "genocide." It isn't simply that these two terms are interrelated, but rather that within a certain mimetic economy, the discourses they *permit to be represented* are ideologically bound.

This is nowhere more visible today than in Israel's invasion of Gaza in response to an "armed incursion" (denounced by some 44 countries as a "terrorist attack," occasioning murder, kidnap & rape) by the Islamic Resistance Movement aka Hamas & its allies on 7 October 2023. With geopolitical alignment strongly affecting the terms in which this conflict has been represented in public discourse, it marked a sensational development when – informed by the disproportionate nature of Israel's response – post-apartheid South Africa brought a case before the International Court of Justice (ICJ) alleging genocide against the Palestinian people. It is within the remit of the ICJ to determine the application of the term "genocide" based upon the meaning given to it by the Convention on the Prevention & Punishment of the Crime of Genocide, adopted by the General Assembly of the United Nations on 9 December 1948. This hasn't prevented western media (including such venerable institutions as the BBC) from seeking to manipulate, if not the legal arguments themselves, then at least the public reception of them. Edward Snowden, the NSA whistleblower who "defected" to Russia in 2013, wrote on social media (13 January, 2024):

> No matter your politics, it should appal you that the media outlets which claim to care the most about "misinformation" suppressed coverage of South Africa's case against the Gaza genocide, but fully covered Israel's defence the next day...

In reference to its ongoing "war against Hamas" (a "designated terrorist organisation"), Israel's defence minister, Yoav Gallant, declared that he had ordered a "complete siege" of Gaza City, that "we will eliminate everything" & that Israel was fighting "human animals." In ordering preventative measures against acts of genocide in Gaza, the ICJ cited this, among other examples, as *prima facie* evidence of a plausible case to be answered by Israel.[13] Israel's reply to these charges had been to argue that its actions (resulting in over 34,000 people killed [roughly 3,000 claimed by Israel to be militants], 775,000 wounded, an undisclosed number arbitrarily detained &, according to UNRWA, more than 2.3 million displaced) constituted self-defence against the "unprecedented attacks" by Hamas on 7 October (resulting in 1,139 military & civilian deaths, of which 364 were attendees at the Re'im Supernova Music Festival, a celebration of "unity & peace").[14] According to Israel's lawyers, it was Hamas, not Israel, whose actions constituted genocide. Indeed, since its foundation, Israel has evoked a state of exception in the matter of its self-defence, since it defines any military attack on itself as *ipso facto* an act of intended erasure of the "Jewish state of Israel" (an expression that reveals how the "Jewish people" & the political entity "Israel" are not only rendered strategically cognate, but how Judaism is actively elided, in the rhetoric of the state – & its laws – with a eugenic "race" principle).[15] In response to the ICJ's ruling, Israeli prime minister, Benjamin Netanyahu, stated "Israel is fighting a just war like no other."

[13] See the full text of the ICJ order indicating provisional measures in the case concerning Application of the Convention on the Prevention & Punishment of the Crime of Genocide in the Gaza Strip (South Africa v. Israel): https://www.icj-cij. org/sites/default/files/case-related/192/192-20240126-ord-01-00-en.pdf. Federal court judge Jeffrey White, hearing a subsequent case in California regarding US military support for Israel, ruled on 2.2.24 "the undisputed evidence before this court comports with the findings of the ICJ & indicates that the current treatment of the Palestinians in the Gaza Strip by the Israeli military may plausibly constitute a genocide in violation of international law." https://www.theguardian.com/ world/2024/feb/01/genocide-gaza-israel-california-court

[14] Reported figures at time of publication (21 April 2024) via www.aljazeera.com

[15] A recurring question in the history of the state of Israel is why did European Jewry seemingly go to their deaths in the Nazi camps "like sheep to the slaughter?" It's a shameful question: shameful because it pretends not to know the answer. Meanwhile, Israel's increasingly extremist leadership exhibits rage at the fact that the Palestinians, forced to live in ghettos of Israel's making, should fight back. Today, Israel's performance of righteous indignation too easily resembles the expunging of a history built on a legacy of Jewish people supposedly *failing to defend themselves.* The over-arching justification for all of Israel's military actions in Palestine – the right of Israel to self-defence – is compensation for *this.*

Poetry as crime

On 2 December, 2023, Nour al-Din Hajjaj, author of *The Gray Ones* (2022) & *Wings That Do Not Fly* (2021), was killed by an Israeli "airstrike"/"terror bombing" on his home in Al-Shujaiyya, shortly after posting on social media:

> This… might be my last message that makes it out to the free world, flying with the doves of peace to tell them that we love life, or at least what life we have managed to live; in Gaza all paths before us are blocked, & instead we're just one tweet or breaking news story away from death.
>
> Anyway, I'll begin.
>
> My name is Nour al-Din Hajjaj, I am a Palestinian writer, I am twenty-seven years old & I have many dreams.
>
> I am not a number & I do not consent to my death being passing news. Say, too, that I love life, happiness, freedom, children's laughter, the sea, coffee, writing, Fairouz, everything that is joyful—though these things will all disappear in the space of a moment.

Kristeva observes that, for Arendt, "only action as narration – & narration as action – can fulfil life in terms of what is 'specifically human' about it."[16] Arendt challenges the notion that poetic work is somehow *remote from life*, insisting rather on the contiguity of poiēsis & a certain *praxis* of human subjectivity.[17] Whether or not this is sufficient to withstand the force of abstraction that reduces the "life as narrative" of those, like Hajjaj, who *insofar as they signify at all to a certain western consciousness* do so as a statistical increment of collateral murder. Like NPCs denied the status of protagonists in this "just war" – a war, allegedly, on "terror" – their narratives exist only in the far margins, among *civilian casualties* deemed, in the cynical rhetoric of those responsible, *unfortunate* but otherwise *unavoidable* (the cast-offs of teleology). Yet more than just the vocabulary of this "tragic view" rings false. During the 2014 "Gaza War" (aka Operation Protective Edge), American critic & proponent of L=A=N=G=U=A=G=E poetry, Marjorie Perloff, wrote on social media in a response to Eugene Ostashevsky,

[16] Kristeva, *Hannah Arendt*, 8.

[17] "It is of this life, *bios* as distinguished from mere *zoē*, that Aristotle said that it 'somehow is a kind of *praxis*.'" Arendt, *The Human Condition*, 97.

The media reporting has been disgusting – nothing but pictures of the "innocent children" in Gaza. First of all, children are NOT innocent; anyone who has ever had children or been around children knows how cruel & mean children can be. Most of the parents of these children are apolitical too so can be classified as "innocent" if you like. The only reason right now that Israelis are not being killed in the same numbers are because they're down in the bomb shelters!

Perloff's intervention belies a wider ideological condition of the War on Terror phenomenon, in which the "innocent" are never innocent but *de facto* "enemy combatants" (minus any dignity conferred by that term under the Geneva Conventions). The narratives of such *de facto* combatants are thus doubly erased: firstly, in the mass of statistics; secondly, as quasi-terrorist propaganda. Implicitly "guilty" of an antisemitism which, like original sin, is seemingly the ontological condition of Israel's "adversaries," Hajjaj's self-testimony is, as it were, made to evoke an *inherently criminal* poetics. The same may just as easily have been said of the diary of Anne Frank. And here we must add a caveat to Arendt's notion of the "banality of evil": for it is in the nature of such an evil that it always projects back upon that which testifies to & against it, in a kind of *righteous indignation*. It's no accident that, in her reflections on the 1960 trial of Adolf Eichmann in Jerusalem, Arendt cast the "architect of the Final Solution" as a kind of mirror-image to the Israeli prosecutor (& Attorney General) Gideon Hausner, as two disfigured versions of the Kantian categorical imperative.

By what means, the terror of rhetoric?
Shortly before his death in 1940, attempting to flee the Nazis, Walter Benjamin wrote: "The current amazement that the things we are experiencing are 'still' possible in the twentieth century is *not* philosophical. This amazement is not the beginning of knowledge – unless it is the knowledge that the view of history which gives rise to it is untenable."[18] In her introduction to the volume in which Benjamin's text posthumously appeared, Arendt observed:

[18] Walter Benjamin, "Theses on the Philosophy of History," *Illuminations*, trans. Harry Zohn (New York: Harcourt, Brace & World, 1968) thesis 8.

> Any period to which its own past has become as questionable as it has to us must eventually come up against the phenomenon of language, for in it the past is contained ineradicably, thwarting all attempts to get rid of it once & for all. The Greek *polis* will continue to exist at the bottom of our political existence – that is, at the bottom of the sea – for as long as we use the word "politics." This is what the semanticists, who with good reason attack language as the one bulwark behind which the past hides – its confusion, as they say – fail to understand. They are absolutely right: in the final analysis all problems are linguistic problems; they simply do not know the implications of what they are saying.[19]

A rhetoric of the impossible discloses itself in an appeal to unrepeatable history. Which isn't to say that past events are deemed beyond the bounds of present or future action. Rather, that the meaning of present & future possibility is itself foreclosed by the burden of history: its ultimate, negative-dialectical counterpart. Not long after Benjamin's death the Shoah came to radicalise this idea, as the manifest "never again" of an historical impossibility transfigured into a teleological force. Since Israel's declaration of independence on 14 May 1948,[20] the systematic murder of 6,000,000 Jews by the Nazis has (by a kind of inescapable necessity) served as the *transcendental signified* of Israel's "state of exception." Such is the singularity of this transcendental signified that the very notions of individual & species falter before it. When Mahmoud Darwish speaks of a poetry of defeat, we need to understand this also as a poetry of metaphysical overwhelm. It is an overwhelm often expressed in quasi-cybernetic terms, of extremely large numbers, the number 6,000,000 to be exact. This monstrous arithmetical regime stands as the counterpart of that zero to which both the individual & the collective are reduced by a totalising programme of erasure present in contemporary discourse under the name *genocide*.[21]

All transcendental signifieds point to a condition that is both radically finite yet open-ended, infinite. If the *meaning* of this infinity & of this finitude opens itself to dispute, its *fact* represents the *ne*

---

[19] Hannah Arendt, "Introduction," *Illuminations*, 49.

[20] Anticipating by seven months the UN's adoption of the Genocide Convention.

[21] The term was first coined by Raphael Lemkin in his 1944 book *Axis Rule in Occupied Europe.*

plus ultra of what must remain, everywhere & always, indisputable. Here the impossible stands in a particular relation to the language of its avowals or disavowals, its *testimonies*, those narratives alone by which its truth is *enacted*, so to speak, in the lives it simultaneously erases & inscribes, in memory to itself, as the "itself" of an unrepeatable, unpresentable singularity. An apocalyptic strain of thought holds that the meaning of such singularity is expressed in the movement of a world historical spirit, a kind of paradoxical "manifest destiny": some New Jerusalem gained at the price of oblivion.[22] Yet the contrary of such apocalypticism also poses a philosophical dilemma. In a letter from Paris dated 1935, Benjamin wrote: "On this planet a great number of civilizations have perished in blood & horror. Naturally, one must wish for the planet that one day it will experience a civilization that has abandoned blood & horror; in fact, I am... inclined to assume that our planet is waiting for this."[23] What kind of "civilisation" affecting a claim over that noun could exist in such a state of self-abandon, if not as a contradiction-in-terms: a civilisation of "defeat," of "manifest destiny" declined, of "self-supersession"? Is such a dissident institution even conceivable, without instantly reverting to the status of an *impossibility*? Utopia, in fewer words? Or not at all, simply the limit of a totalising rhetoric that seeks, even at the point of expiring, to aggregate to itself the only exception permissible?

Prague, February 2024

---

[22] This apocalyptic tone is not a recent adoption of philosophy. From its origin, philosophy has always needed to contend with the absence of history before it can assert what it "is." Constructed upon the analogy of forensic anatomy, the "meaning of history" assumes a retrospective character, emblematised by Benjamin's Angelus Novus: that no species of being can be fully grasped until after it's dead. This, philosophy does by substitution & imitation; that is to say, by self-substitution on the one hand & by a kind of morbid posthumous reconstruction on the other (the future in the rearview mirror). History, as the doppelganger of reason itself, is made to labour on under a kind of Frankenstein syndrome for the sake of an ultimate "end" that must, by the same imperative that demanded it, be perpetually deferred.

[23] Qtd in Arendt, "Introduction," 38.

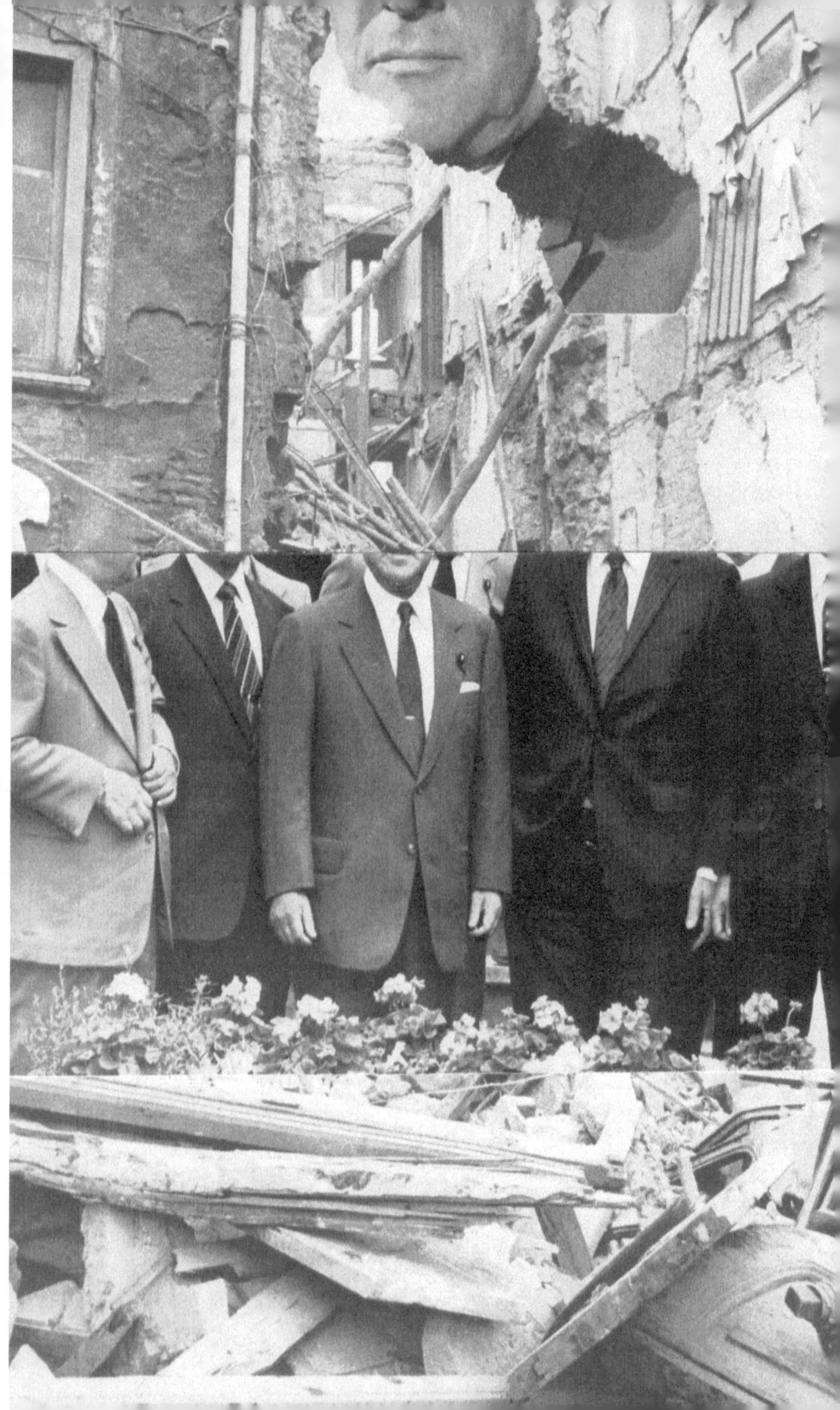

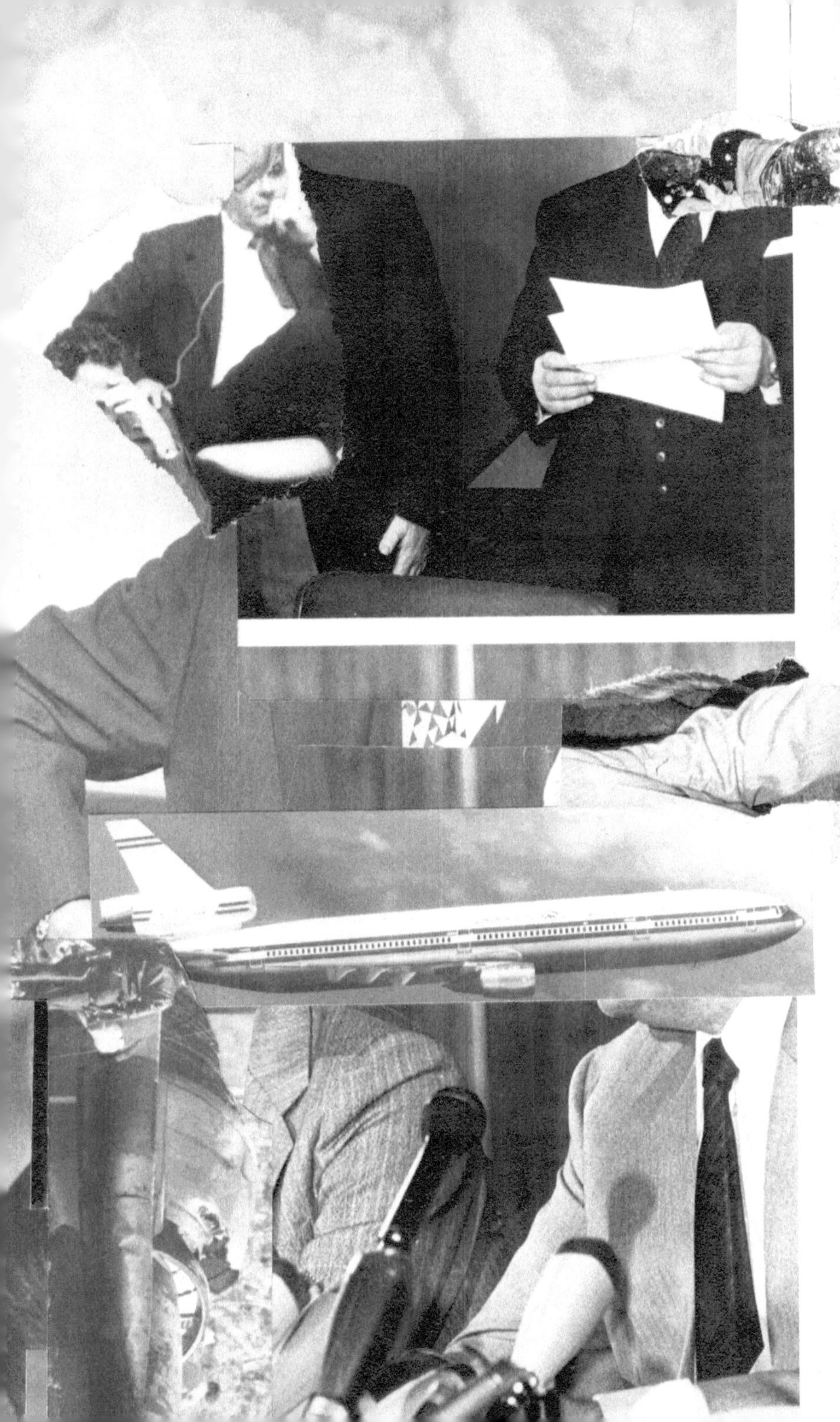

FEASTS OF UNRULE

[AVANT-TRANS]

Theodor Adorno's often cited pronouncement that "To write poetry after Auschwitz is an act of barbarism" has to be taken as true in two ways. It is true, first, because what happened at "Auschwitz" (taken both literally & metonymically, standing for itself, for the other death camps, & also for what has occurred at numerous other atrocity sites throughout this century) is (& must remain) incomprehensible (literally unthinkable) & therefore, in the most vicious way, "meaningless" – that is, it is not possible to make or discover meaning anywhere in the context of Auschwitz & moreover, ever since Auschwitz (i.e., henceforth in human history) everything exist in that context. All possibilities for meaning have been suspended or crushed. But Adorno's statement can be interpreted in another sense, not as a condemnation of the attempt "after Auschwitz" to write poetry, but, on the contrary, as a challenge & behest to do so. The word "barbarism," as it comes to us from the Greek *barbaros*, means "foreign" – that is, "not speaking the same language" (*barbaros* being an onomatopoeic imitation of babbling) – & such is precisely the task of poetry: *not to speak the same language as Auschwitz*. Poetry after Auschwitz must indeed be barbarian; it must be foreign to the cultures that produce atrocities. As a result, the poet must assume a barbarian position, taking a creative, analytic, & often oppositional stance, occupying (& being occupied by) foreignness – by the barbarism of strangeness.

(Lyn Hejinian, "Barbarism")

Poetry dances on a rose

In Book X of *The Republic*, Plato outlines a means of rapprochement between poetry & philosophy in the "ancient quarrel" over mimēsis.

This rapprochement appears as a countermovement to the often-discussed "banishment" or "expulsion" of poetry from the ideal polis ("the rejection of imitative poetry, which certainly ought not to be received" [X.595]).[1] In Stephen Halliwell's account, Plato's subsequent recuperation of poetry *for* philosophy is symptomatic of "an unsolved, abiding problem" rather than "the unequivocal outcome of an irreconcilable conflict."[2] In place of a movement of negation & sublation, Plato's dialectical turn is marked by ambivalence. For Halliwell, such ambivalence is encoded in Plato's text itself, whereby the arguments against poetry are, so to speak, programmed in advance to *fail*. Yet what this failure entails is nowhere clearly given in Plato's text, beyond the characteristic employment of rhetorical figures & the allusion to poetry's seduction, its magical charm, its capacity to enchant philosophy, & – somewhat tellingly – *philosophy's own predisposition to enchantment* ("the childish love of her which captivates the many" [X.608]). The task assigned to philosophy, here, is thus to enact a *dis*enchantment – one which is first & foremost *self-directed* – & to preserve a relation to poetry which does not, as in the analogy of the Cave, risk enslavement to illusion. This *philosophical prophylaxis*, having first of all taken the form of a "reasonable" exclusion of the imitative arts, now reverts to "reason" itself: that is to say, to the force of reasoned argument as a relation to truth. "Let us assure our sweet friend & the sister arts of imitation," Plato writes, "that if she will only prove her title to exist in a well-ordered State we shall be delighted to receive her." Such "proof" being to construct a defence before the tribunal of reason (i.e. of those who speak in philosophy's name) & to enlist advocates otherwise permitted "to speak in prose on her behalf" [X.607].

Let's suppose that the name belonging to this philosophical prophylaxis is *translation*.

---

[1] Cf *Phaedrus*, wherein the autonomy of the (poetic) logos is posed as a liability to the ideological centrism of the *state of reason*: an errancy that threatens to infect the entire *system of meaning*. The movement of expulsion mirrors in this sense the decentredness that the errant logos itself represents, in an effort both to forestall but also contain it. Hence writing/poetry must (if reason is to retain its hegemonic relation to it) be resisted/suppressed as irredeemably foreign/alien/parasitic/hostile/a species of succubus/the barbarian at the gates/the wolf at the door; yet, also, & *in no way paradoxically*, be incorporated (that is to say, comprehended).

[2] Stephen Halliwell, "Antidotes & Incantations: Is there a Cure for Poetry in Plato's *Republic*," *Plato & the Poets* eds. P. Destree & F.-G. Herrmann (Leiden: Brill, 2011) 260.

If the "abiding problem" of philosophy, to borrow Halliwell's expression, is the relationship of its own discourse to mimēsis, it nevertheless calls this problem "poetry" or "the imitative arts." But poetry is more than philosophy's misrecognised doppelgänger: it is the site of a certain *subjection to ideology*. If the zone of exclusion (beyond the polis) equates to a zone of *barbarism*, poetry equates to the barbaric yawp of a non-subject deprived of "logos." Yet insofar as translation is enlisted as a strategy of extrusion & *concentration*, this subjection is not the *subjection of poetry to the rule of reason* it has so often been asserted, but the inverse: reason itself as subject to a certain *translation-effect* traced through the locus of *unreason* (a-logos): the barbarian other on whom it is fixated.

Plato's gambit here is to render the primordial mythopoetics of the polis foreign to it, *in the name of reason*, by means of which the polis is enabled to transcend its own primitivism for the promise of modernity – played out in a drama of recuperation between a new "state poetry" (that submits to translation) & a certain "non-poetry" (that refuses) – the irony of which is always double-edged.[3] This may be characterised by two movements, or two moments, of transition in the dialectic, marked by: 1. an incommensurable "difference" that here *demands* the translation of poetic unreason into the prose of reason, *in the first place*; 2. what may be called the irreducible "remainder" of such a translation, *produced* by it yet forever *incomprehensible* to it.

More: in Plato's solicitation of translation (& of the *trans* more generally), reason unconsciously inscribes its own subjectivisation *in advance* – as what Lacan calls "subjection to the signifier" or what Derrida calls both the "prior possibility" & simultaneous "impossibility" of *translation as such.* Philosophy avoids appearing to be a mere *residuum* of poetics stripped of indeterminacy, ambivalence, metaphor – *by way of the prophylactic operation of*

---

[3] The teleology of the State of Reason is a "play of mirrors," between two barbarisms & two solipsisms, born of the renunciation of poiēsis only to end in the mythodrama of an "impossible" self-knowledge: mimēsis of mimēsis. As in Adorno: "The critique of culture is confronted with the last stage in the dialectic of culture & barbarism: to write a poem after Auschwitz is barbaric, & that corrodes also the knowledge which expresses why it has become impossible to write poetry today." (Theodor Adorno, "An Essay on Cultural Criticism and Society," *Prisms*, trans. Samuel & Shierry Weber (Cambridge, Mass.: MIT Press, 1955) 34.

the trans – by seeking to represent the *trans* as a movement of *subsumption*. Poetry, insofar as it ceases to be what it is & instead speaks in the *prose of reason*, is subsumed into philosophy, which for its part pretends that the entire theatre of this "ancient quarrel" is not itself *metaphor* (which is to say, the site of its own *incomprehension*: the fact remains that reason *does not know what poetry "is,"* despite every effort to establish the terms of a translational schema in which poetry is objectified & philosophy is designated as the unique recipient of its transmission). It's not for nothing that Plato concludes Book X by reversioning Homer's account of Odysseus in Hades as philosophical bildungsroman, in which translation (substituting for hermeneutic) is implicitly bound to reason's challenge of passing "safely over the river of Forgetfulness" [X.621], anticipating its Hegelian sequel as the *freedom* arising from the self-conscious task of unforgetting, which reveals itself as a becoming-conscious of reason itelf *as self-subjection*.

Reason is only what it *does* (Hegel)
To proceed directly to the subject at hand, we may say that the question of *rapprochement* between "poetry" & the "well-ordered State" – which is to say, of *recuperation* & *institutionalisation* – directly anticipates the question, par excellence, of "revolutionary art" & the socalled "avantgarde." That is to say: insofar as Plato's dialectical gesture mirrors the antinomy construed in Peter Bürger's schema, between the "historical avantgarde" & its *imitation, translation* or spectral counterpart in the "neo-." And just as, in Plato, poetry is intended to be entrapped within an impossible task (the necessity & impossibility of translation), so in Bürger the neoavantgarde signifies a *détournement* of the original force of the avantgarde's institutional critique *by precisely those forces of institutionalisation with which it becomes fixated & into which it becomes absorbed.*

In Plato, a certain strategy of *mimēsis* is brought to bear upon the "problem" of the "imitative arts," here reduced to the task of reflecting the self-image of the "well-ordered state" (reason or *the institution* per se). And yet such a strategy – one which purports to issue from a position of ideological strength – gives rise to a seemingly unanticipated countermovement, which is that of a "solicitation" (though in reality this may be a sign of institutional frisson or jouissance: Plato's enchantment; the neoavantgarde as theatre of institutional self-subversive play). Specifically, the "solicitation" of the *trans* is both a call to translation (as neutralisation of meaning within a given ideological framework) & its destabilising potential (by introducing an irreducible element, generative of structural perturbations within that framework). At the same time, no such solicitation would be possible without a "prior possibility," as Derrida notes, through which both Plato's & Bürger's schemas reveal themselves to be *internally translated* in advance. It isn't simply that reason or institutionalisation "contain" internal contradictions, rather they themselves mirror the propositions they bring to bear upon their objects.

Reason in Plato *is* the ideology of mimēsis: institutionalisation in Bürger *is* the "dream of the avantgarde" – but it is the *institution's* dream which is reflected in Bürger's thought, just as poetry is philosophy's "dream" in Plato, conjured for reason's perpetual delectation in a masochistic spectacle of submission & abasement. In Plato, the *seduction* of poetry is prophylactised like a peepshow through a two-way mirror. In Bürger, criticism is the voyeur, & the striptease – like those conjurations in Plato's cave – is pure travesty (not because the avantgarde for Bürger has ceased to pose dangers & therefore has become *inauthentic*, but because its *contemplation* by a self-proclaimed "theory of the avantgarde" is *risk-averse*: it itself is an *imitation* of critical risk-taking & finds its objects in the domain of the *spectral*).

What's left to say about an "avantgardism" whose fetishistic reinventions, renewals, recyclings of domesticated barbarism appear, in the long wake of the 20th century, to be nothing more than the ambivalent performance of a *translation, transition, transposition* – of this "irreducible object" into that "generative procedure" & always *after the fact*? As both subjection-to-institutional-power & as edifying spectacle-of-power's-insufficiency? As "history in action" dancing to the tune of alienated *poiēsis* raising its fist in the air but only when there's a camera in the room?[4]

Liège, November 2023

[4] See G.W.F. Hegel, *The Philosophy of History*, trans. J. Sibree (New York: Dover, 1956) §342-§343.

1. INCIPIT PARODIA

> The world is purely parodic... each thing seen is the parody of
> another, or is the same thing in a deceptive form...
>
> (Georges Bataille, "The Solar Anus")

Perhaps artificial intelligence (socalled) will finally do for "literature"
in the 21st century what photography, in the 19th, did for "painting."
No Turing Test need distinguish between them: the dross of mimēsis
is always already a product of ideological machinery, one that has
never required a pretence to autonomous action, having ruled over
the field of representation from ancient times.

From the "beginning," the stakes in this revolution-of-the-word
have been nothing less than the mass-manufacture of (political)
discourse: the logistics of power.

The "sacred" texts of the monotheisms, plagiarised from
Zoroaster, assert as their copyright an entire cosmology. But a
monopoly over textual production – which is to say, the production
of social meaning – is called utopianism in the hands of "avantgarde"
fringe elements. Power is concerned with the fringe only as an
object of rhetorical capture, exclusion or isolation, so as to occupy
the central ground & to do so as if *by necessity*, which is to say,
automatically & *absolutely*.

The invention of writing (in Plato's retrospective, self-parodying
critique) revealed a mechanistic universe in prototype. Its paradox
was to represent not the triumph of reason but reason's ultimate
detachment from the human idea. Language would henceforth no

longer be reducible to a *technē politikē* but would inscribe the entire field of political possibility (& impossibility). In it, the law of genre would achieve its apotheosis in generic universality.

"Literature" doesn't exist as a separate region of discourse but is contiguous with discourse in its entirety. It is on account of this that the operations of power are not only *not* alien to it, but are in fact represented at every point within it, such that literature may be considered ideology's doppelganger.

Teleology is the bildungsroman of power

Beginning with the question of literature: as a general status of writing & an amplification of the relation of writing to power. The aesthetic notion of autonomy *within a system* & *as an ambivalent relation to that system*. It is literature's "modernity," according to a more or less recent intervention by Jacques Rancière, that both emerges from & (thus) reveals this latent *indifference* – the "democratic availability" of writing being a derivation of a capacity inscribed in the figure of a "mute" or "dead letter" circulating within "the rules & hierarchies of representation," which in turn threaten to produce the collapse of that system & "of the whole regime of meaning."[1]

Theory, in this formulation, is conceived as the responsibility of a "critique" founded in the radical *ambivalence* of such a literature (by operating within & across the opposed ways "of linking meaning & action" vis-à-vis "the *power* of framing a common world"). Hence ideology is conceived as literature's other: that which – by a play of mirrors – appears to contain it ("literature") within a fictional field (as reflection or illusion), while being itself founded upon this very fictionality (as system of universal-hypothesis: the illusion of something that stands *behind the mirror*, operating it).

It's not for nothing that Derrida insists that "writing & power never work separately, however complex the laws, the system, or the links of their collusion may be... what is astonishing is not writing's power but what comes, as if from within structure, to limit it by a powerlessness or an effacement."[2] The apparent

[1] Jacques Rancière, "The Politics of Literature," trans. Julie Rose, *SubStance* 33.1 (2004): 10-24.
[2] Jacques Derrida, "Scribble (writing-power")," trans. Cary Plotkin, *Yale French Studies*, no. 58 (1979): 117–47.

inverse of this is the notion that writing "brings about not only a decomposition or destruction," as Deleuze says, but also "the invention of a new language within language" – that is to say, *within* the field of ideology.

This *invention* (of a language-within-language) is always a *pharmakon*: "a foreign language cannot be hollowed out in one language without language as a whole [ideology as a whole] being... pushed to a limit."[3] The translation of the one to (or "within") the other – of writing as literature, theory, ideology – is always a state of being *out-of-joint*, the temporality of a "struggle," the *(in)différance* of a writing that arrives in advance of itself: as the (ambivalent) thought of a to-come; of the ever-displaced future of power's dream of endlessness.

No literary theory without a theory of the state

Two concepts of "literature" thus appear to exist side-by-side & virtually within the same space: that of literature as what Althusser called Ideological State Apparatus & its apparent contrary, literature as subversion of state ideology.[4] The first associates with the "institutionalisation" of culture – though its premise, of course, is that culture, in its essential meaning, is already the discourse of the state; the second associates with the avantgardist notion of autonomy, not as an assertion of "art-for-art's-sake" but as a critical orientation towards the state, founded in a constitutive alienation from it ("art," here, is that which occurs *despite* & *exterior to* the operations of the state). One implies a teleological immanence, the other a "dialectical struggle." One pursues an appearance of homogeneity, the other asserts itself as radically heterogeneous. This, at least, is the dualism most familiar to modern literary theory: a dualism that is as much a product as a description of that relation between language & power otherwise known as cultural modernity.[5]

---

3 Gilles Deleuze, "Literature & Life," trans. Daniel W. Smith & Michael A. Greco, *Critical Inquiry* 23, no. 2 (1997): 225–30.

4 The question I begin with is the relation between literature & the state, between a theory of literature & a theory of the state, not one theory or another but a general field of implication that arises from the proximity of these terms, literature & state, & what goes on between & within them, in the space of a "comparison."

5 If modernity is characterised by successive dualisms – "schismogeneses" – this may be symptomatic of its relation to that phenomenon of rationalist systematisation

There are antecedents for this, periods in which literature has been formalised into particular species of ideological object: whether in service to a given ideology, or in opposition to it. In general, whether it chooses to or not, literature has always been bound to considerations of state: we do not need to look very far to find examples. Virtually without exception, the ideological "content" of this subjection is as much formal as topical: subjection to laws of genre, of rhetoric, prosody, grammar, etc., but also of an aesthetic morality that expresses itself through the exclusion of polysemy, ambiguity, ambivalence, strange metaphors & other deviations from a semantics of "truth." The archetype for this is no doubt Plato's *Republic*, itself an illustration of a literature at the service of the state: its enemy is the poetry of "unreason."

What occurs, then, in this zone of a between-two-literatures? The one, a formalised expression of a philosophy of state, of reason, of a pure hermeneutic; the other its contrary, or rather its *adversary*. There is a sense in which what we call "comparative literature" must imply, first & foremost, the contestation of this doubled & duplicitous term "literature" – & in so doing, to question the assumed standpoint of *comparison* as such, between one notional "corpus" & another.[6] Such a standpoint will always have risked devolving into the singularity of an enstatement: the point-of-view, for example, of a Cartesianism, of an "objective" reason, supervising the divided, yet for this same reason totalisable, "field" of literature. How, then, is it possible to speak of a "comparative literature" without affirming precisely those hegemonic relations that comparativism – by virtue of opening itself to the "other" – might be assumed to scrutinise & critique?[7]

that called itself the European enlightenment: an "incomplete project," to abuse Habermas' phraseology, because *constitutively incompletable*. Modernism may simply be – like Gödel's theorem – the articulation of this incompleteness.

[6] There is another sense of "comparison," of course, one that implies not a difference between terms but a difference without terms: literature as a differential body through which the terms of its contestations, its institutionalisation, its nationalisation, are in fact brought into being *as an effect of literature* & not vice versa.

[7] A "comparative literature" that is simply a point-of-view from one national corpus onto those of "others" amounts to little more than a reification of the ideology of the state under the guise of pluralism. There is no equivalence between such a pluralism & the polymorphous perversity of texts like *Makbara*. Such a text cannot be "orientated" within the binary relation of a point-of-view directed at foreign objects:

A people with no poetry is a defeated people[8]

When Mahmoud Darwish asked if it is possible for the defeated to possess a poetry of "their own," he was asking two things: Is it possible for poetry to be separate from the hegemony of the nation state & from the odyssey of an impossible nostalgia (i.e., that poetry must *belong*)? Or is it *only* possible for a poetry that isn't groomed to officiate at the ceremonies of power to exist in a state of "defeat" (of failure, of inadequacy, of redundancy, of insignificance, etc.): a poetry on the underside of nation-state triumphalism; a poetry under a perpetual state-of-siege? But more: If literature is born in a state of hegemonic relations, ought "poetry" itself be understood more generally as precisely what threatens to *escape* a hegemonic rationale & not merely as what is *excluded* by it? Yet if, merely to exist, poetry must, from the viewpoint of power, be *a priori* defeated, indentured to the state, "mute" (i.e. incomprehensible) unless *called upon* (granted permission) *to speak,* nevertheless the opposite may be closer to the truth: poetry as the quintessential foreigner, the *Geist* or *spectre* haunting the institution of literature, both *at its frontiers* & *from within?*

If, in Plato, poetry is made to appear doubly defeated *in order to speak* – by betraying itself, its own autonomy, its own recusance – what can be said of the very disproportionate array of ideological forces required to affect this "defeatism"?[9] This might indicate that not only does the ideological state apparatus not cover the entire discursive field, but that its spectacle of power (that which it calls "culture") is phantasmatic. To the extent that power seeks to recuperate the discourses of its others, this recuperative movement,

its foreignness *is* its orientation, which "infects" any point-of-view adopted with relation to it. Moreover, its foreignness is *cognizant,* in advance, of the "point-of-view" as such, since it itself represents – insofar as it "represents" anything – both the traversal & travesty of the "literary object." The fascination that it exercises arises from within the very space, or nonspace, from which any comparison must emerge: that is to say, the space of a nonspace.

[8] Mahmoud Darwish, A *State of Siege, trans.* Munir Akash, Daniel Abdal-hayy Moore (New York: Syracuse University Press, 2010).

[9] Recently, a movement in "radical poetics" has once again raised the spectre of defeatedness as a precondition of revolutionary thought & poetic action. One of its points of reference has been the "failed" events of 1968, among others, treated as an "incomplete project" that literature has been complicit in consigning to the dustbin of history. Can this still be discounted as mere romanticism? As a kind of empty neoavantgardism?

too, may be merely reflexive, hyperbolic, paranoiac: moreover, the very notion of recuperation points to the fact that power is not only open at its borders, but is constantly traversed by what it only nominally limits & subjects.[10] Darwish's question thus needs to re-stated: Can there be *only* a defeated poetry?

Let us be clear that when we speak of a "defeat" in this sense, we are speaking of a radicalism: the poetics of defeat, here, is a radical poetics.

But what is it actually possible for a "literary theory" to say about such a radical poetics that does not, in advance, admit defeat?[11] Is "literary theory" in any way equipped to comprehend a radical poetics as anything but an *anecdote*, for example, of social reform or as a *simulation* of insurrectionary force ("avantgardism")? What must occur to the institution of "literary theory" in order for a radical poetics to be conceivable by it other than in terms of the language of power itself arrayed as if *in opposition?*[12]

A radical poetics cannot begin with a challenge thrown in the face of power by those who are merely impotent, or let us say "defeated": rather, it begins in the experience of a discrepancy between the grandiose claims of power – under the rubric of Culture, Literature, Identity, & so on – & the very tenuous nature of those institutions themselves: a tenuousness made all the more evident by a compulsive, even paranoiac need to "sublimate" everything that calls them into question.[13]

---

[10] A discourse of power that otherwise possesses nothing but the "fact" of itself, an *empty signifier* in an imaginary relation to a fictional *real*.

[11] Can it only be judged against a positivistic diagnosis or programmatic alternative to the present World Order? That is expected to constitute a call to action or instigate responsible change? That would necessarily falter before the spectre of revolutionary violence in the actual overthrow of the state?

[12] How, then, can a radical poetics escape reduction to being just another trope in the dialectics of power itself? The Platonic tactic is to present truth-to-power as *a priori*, & to demonstrate this by a perpetual recuperative movement orientated at overcoming the threat of mystification & obscurantism posed by poetic language. Accepting this proposition means accepting the secondary, dissimulative status of poetry vis-à-vis a "prose of reason" given priority in relation to truth. A radical poetics would imply something entirely other: to begin with, the actual *insufficiency* of any socalled dialectics of power: whose truth is exposed as *conditional upon* the subjugation of poetic language. Which is to say, upon the apparent omnipotence of the "dialectical" procedure – in other words, of recuperation.

[13] The oft-lamented institutionalisation of the avantgarde is just one example of this. Yet it accomplishes relatively little to say that the institutional co-option of the

The real power dynamic of institutionalisation stems from the fact that its adversary is never merely symbolic but poses, in some way, a real threat & must be really defeated. Plato's exclusion of poetry from the ideal polis isn't trivial. Poetry is accused of representing unreason itself, & so must be excluded from the philosophical state for the sake of its political & social health, an action which is presented as the epitome of reason. Yet being reasonable, the state also permits poetry to plead its case for re-inclusion, but only in the language of prose.

It is the charade of "reasonableness" here that shows the state not as *enlightened* but rather *insufficient,* & while its offer of appeal before the tribunal of reason may appear cynical & opportunistic, it also exposes a certain desperation: reason is not omniscient, instead it is revealed to be an *ideological prophylactic.* This again recalls Darwish's argument that the defeated prosper from the prestige of their vanquishers, who it envies; while it is the vanquisher who in turn erects monuments to itself on the basis of the prestige of the vanquished, who it despises.

Such tendencies are not artefacts of modernity or of the emergence of what we understand today as nation states: the classical & preclassical worlds are rife with purloined literary corpuses, religions, epistemologies, entire plundered cultural edifices often only thinly disguised. Yet this should also alert us to the relativism of this discourse.[14] But something is amiss here if

avantgarde, or of a radical poetics, is nothing other than a kind of self-embarrassed effort at pretending to a benevolent yet totalising authority, even when such an attempt may be shown to represent the opposite. If the prestige of the institution rests upon the paradoxical necessity of both enlarging & diminishing the prestige of its erstwhile adversary, this by itself does nothing to subvert the real power of institutionalisation. As Napoleon famously said, power is never ridiculous, no matter how much the powerless may like to say so: the fact that they say so, rather than seize power itself, is as indicative of this state of affairs as anything.

[14] The poetic text that Plato's ideal polity most desired to subjugate was that of Homer: whereas, for Darwish, it is the *Iliad* that serves as the source code of a western cultural hegemony transposed – against the background of centuries of pogroms, exile, & the Nazi holocaust – onto the state ideology of modern Israel. And if the Virgil's *Aeneid* takes the side of Homer's vanquished, so as to provide a creation myth for Rome, it isn't to *avow* a poetics of the defeated, but to underwrite the Augustan imperialist narrative with a historical conceit of historical revenge upon the Greek world – revenge, that is to say, for having predefined its cultural reference points (including the ideology of reason): an Oedipal gesture of recuperation *par excellence* in which "history" is merely an alibi. Whether it is falsified history or not is beside

the "poetry of defeat," which is to say a landless poetry – a poetry of displacement, of exile & unbelonging – is understood purely & simply as a genre of historical resentment: a lament to be rehearsed down the generations until such a time as the tables are turned or fortunes are reversed in some literary Promised Land. Such an immiserated poetry would be little more than the kitsch of disempowerment, just as one may say that the artefacts of "official culture" are the kitsch of power.[15]

Culture is the paranoiac ego of "civilisation"?

"Fighting alienation from totally alienated positions"[16] is how Juan Goytisolo expresses this apparent double-bind in one of his lesser-known works of anti-literature, *Makbara*.[17] Like Darwish, Goytisolo poses questions about a defeated poetry, to which the work itself is the effective response. *Makbara* sets out to affect a travesty of a

the point, what matters is that subjugation & expropriation are made to appear *just*: pseudo-retribution becomes pseudo-rectification.

[15] It is necessary, therefore, to consider what it must mean for a poetry – in general & not merely in its historical particularities – to be "defeated" in a more fundamental, constitutive sense, as in the constitutive "alienation" of the individual in Marx & Freud, for example, or in Rimbaud. There is a tendency to treat the Rimbaudian formula "JE est une autre" as mere subjective tropism, the romantic self-intoxication of the "outsider" poet, as camouflage for the political impotence bestowed by a society organised along lines of subtle authoritarianism, masquerading by turns as "liberal" & "indifferent." The glibness of this view is analogous to that of the avantgarde as a marriage of convenience between frustrated communards & the 1863 Salon des Refusés. Peter Bürger's *Theory of the Avant-Garde* sums this up with the observation that any subversion of the identitarian sub-routines of the state merely risks concretising them, though this is somewhat beside the point. The real business is how such contingencies are employed to serve *post hoc propter hoc* as causalities in the neutralision of a radical poetics: for example, how the avantgarde in Bürger is held *accountable* for the processes of institutionalisation it critiques.

[16] Juan Goytisolo, *Makbara*, trans. Helen Lane (London: Serpent's Tail 1993) 120.

[17] An unruly assemblage of 16 texts, each characterised by syntactic & grammatical fluidity & superfluity; typographic idiosyncrasies (decapitalisation, enjambment); persistently evasive narrative positions, genders, ethnicities, subjectivities; first-second-third person, singular & plural; monologue, dialogue, polylogue; heterogeneous & impure "genres" suspended between or produced across languages (Spanish, French, Moroccan Arabic, Riff, Tamazight, Tachelhit); polymorphous tropic effects amplified at the level of the socalled schema & vice versa (like the flapping of a butterfly's wing, or the sardonic flutter of a transsexual's overly mascaraed eyelash); polymorphous perversities of those antisocial & unsocialisable aspects of "meaning" that are irreducible to, or irredeemable as, an ideological state apparatus. It goes without saying that *Makbara* is very much aware of the provocation it itself represents to the forces of aesthetic morality, for whom such deviations are "haram."

travesty: "a parody that mirrors in reverse the agitation, the frenzy, the commotion of operations" of the paranoiac corporate-state.[18] Goytisolo's text is grounded in a refusal to accept the terms of "identity" that form the basis of Platonic ideology (that the speaker must identify with the truth s/he speaks, etc.), instead *Makbara* presents a narrator whose situation is constantly elided: "I, the European halaiquí who have told you this story, assuming different voices & roles in turn, making the characters fly from one continent to the other."[19]

In a 1984 interview with Julio Ortega, Goytisolo observed: "And it's true that my own birth as a writer coincides in fact with the destruction of my literature, of the literary moulds which in routine fashion I took from tradition."[20] Goytisolo – whose own "moral, social, ideological & sexual exile" from Franco's Spain (spent mostly in Tangier & Marrakech) was in large part caused by an increasingly political stance with regard to language *separate from the claims of national/cultural identity* – insisted that "an expatriate lives generally in a state of anguished isolation. But, this very state of marginality is favoured toward the affirmation of his own ideas, liberated in this way from the hypnosis, from the taboos & the blackmail demanded of him by the society in which he lived," since it is in his discourse that the writer's identity resides. "The creator of 'discourse' changes his voice, & in that manner changes his skin." And by virtue of being a "mere" linguistic character, as some would say, he becomes "an authentic man without a country."

As if to say, in order to *write*, first one must become a foreigner, to discover the foreignness that has inhabited them all along. And this perspective, however paradoxical it seems, is only possible *because of a constitutive alienation & estrangement.* In his reflection on this question – *Masks of Identity* (Señas de identidad, published in Mexico City, 1966), *Juan the Landless* (Juan sin tierra, 1975) & *Makbara* (1980; both published in Barcelona) – Goytisolo pursued a new & audacious elaboration on "novelistic" form in the radical tradition of Cervantes, Joyce & Genet – whose resonances can also be detected among contemporary works like Manuel Puig's *La*

[18] *Makbara* 251.
[19] *Makbara* 239.
[20] Published in the Summer 1984 edition of *The Review of Contemporary Fiction.*

traición de Rita Hayworth (1968) & *Pubis Angelical* (1979), Cabrera Infante's *Tres Tristes Tigres* (1971) & *La Habana para un Infante Difunto* (1979), Severo Sarduy's *Cobra* (1972) & *Maitreya* (1978), Hubert Fichte's *Detlevs Imitationen* (1971), Clarence Major's *Reflex & Bone Structure* (1975), Ignácio Brandão's *Zero* (1979) & Reinaldo Arenas's Pentagonia trilogy, among others.

Goytisolo, who viewed the novel as a "cannibalistic form" able, like Pound's "ragbag of history," to incorporate everything, considered his own writing therefore to be a concertedly *treasonous act* against the "conceptual tyranny of genre." For Goytisolo, such treason wasn't an *acte gratuit*, but a writerly responsibility, accorded through the heterogeneous experience of language, whereas to acquiesce to the injunctions of an experientially-deformative "realism" or retreat into unworldly "fictionising" would amount to the worst kind of culpability: the negation of writing. "A writer," he insisted, "who is unaware of the movements in poetics & linguistics seems to me an anachronism in today's world. The writer can't abandon himself simply to inspiration, & feign innocence vis-à-vis language, because language is never innocent." An avid reader of Joyce & Sterne in the original, Goytisolo's work stands as a major rebuke to the dogmatic anti-modernism, anti-internationalism & anti-experimentalism of a "globalised" culture industry, whose universality it exposes as a confidence trick: doctrine imposed upon the supposed mental capacities of "newly imported slaves" (as a group of ideologues in *Juan the Landless* characterise it), who are made to toil for this neo-imperial master narrative while performing their "otherness" as literary sub-species.

("It's absurd," Goytisolo has said elsewhere, "to make distinctions between national literatures.")[21]

In *Makbara*, the monotheism of the author-figure is devolved onto the figure of the *halaiquí*, or ritual storyteller, borrowing a Swahili term for "crowd," derived from Arabic, *ḵalīqa*, "creature, creation." This authorial narrator is both a "creature" & one who "creates," whose "name" – per the Book of Mark – is quite literally "legion." The halaiquí can be understood as the antithesis of the

<hr>

[21] Juan Goytisolo & J.S. Tennant, "Interview with Juan Goytisolo," *The White Review* (November 2014): https://www.thewhitereview.org/feature/interview-with-juan-goytisolo/

46

singular, of the sacred, of Platonic truth, belonging rather to the heterologous, the transgressive & profane, indeed the *vulgar*. Moreover, the halaiquí represents a fundamental *différance* in(to) which the logos does not "fall" but rather by which it is *constituted*.

In such a way, *Makbara* may be read as a Babelian allegory of the paradox which lies at the heart of all comparativism: as both corpus & anti-corpus. The halaiquí will not be normalised, methodised, systematised, bound by the "prose of reason." This criminal body isn't subject to committal, but is that which commits itself, as when Sartre speaks of a "committed literature" – though decidedly not in the manner in which Sartre intended. What would it mean, here, to *commit* literature? To what extent is the situation of Goytisolo's text resonant with that of, say, Genet? And what if the "crime" were precisely in the incapacity of the law – of reason, genre, etc. – to classify it? A perverse textual body irredeemable by virtue of refusing to become *literature*?[22]

What can the status of such a text be within the framework of a literature grounded in the idea of the state? And what happens to the meaning of "comparativism" in the face of such an irreducible "otherness"? This isn't a rhetorical question: like Rimbaud, the work of "disordering" that is the driving force in Goytisolo's writing is never gratuitous. To Rimbaud's "JE est un autre" Goytisolo adds "je cherche une *orientation*."[23] And if Goytisolo's "I" is a transgendered chaos agent, in whom the concept of orientation is "non-binary," its linguistic actions are likewise deconstructive, a "disordering of the senses" as a deconstruction of the law of genre, etc. Moreover, this deconstruction remains close to its object, the "high-cultural" artefacts of a bureaucratised "enlightenment" & in particular their didactic, pseudo-naturalism, which within a colonial framework can only appear (beyond the most limited of myopic viewpoints) as a *travesty* of "reasonableness."

Makbara's "irrational" topology designates a zone outside the socio-colonial dichotomies, imbued with "the vitality of a great

---

[22] Like the *corps délectable* of the Maghrebi transexual in chapter 7, wreaking havoc in a Parisian *salon du mariage* ("tu as vu, papa? la dame n'a pas rasé sa barbe!" [*Makbara* 91] – a punning allusion also to the figure of the "barbarian," but also the "Berber," as (both Western & Arab) colonialism's "other(s)."

[23] *Makbara* 98 – emphasis added

meltingpot."[24] But Goytisolo's mapping of one vision of a cultural meltingpot onto another (correspondingly alien) one – of the Sahara, for example, onto the Parisian cosmopolis – represents more than a superposition of two conflicting modes of modernity, two comparativisms (one decentred by successive postcolonialisms – Phoenician, Roman, Arab, Portuguese, Spanish, French – the other, the imploded centre of a still-ongoing colonial & neocolonial project whose cultural force has nevertheless migrated into the realm of myth & virtualism; one, constitutively heterogeneous, the other paranoiacally driven to incorporate its "others" so as to maintain, even in the form of self-contradiction, an illusory monopoly on cultural capital[25]). Here, to reprise Darwish's term, are thus also two modes of a poetics of "defeat." Where the "Saharan" emerges from what we might call a topological resistance to hegemony, in its various historical manifestations, the "cosmopolitan" emerges from a crisis within the discourse of history subsumed within a certain *polity* of reason.[26] But if Goytisolo's melting-pot evokes a "disordering,"[27] this is because it signifies a place in which identity[28] – as an ego-psychology of the state (reason) – is dissolved & re-

[24] *Makbara* 134. This topological involution both produces & subverts a state literature, & which thereby would also define "the state" of literature in general.

[25] The injunction we historically encounter against the translation of sacred texts, contested almost universally (though not synchronously) in the name of the vernacular, ironically becomes the template of a most conventionalised "national corpus," translated half by race-myth & half by a kind of historical materialism. Yet the work of "comparison" is itself premised upon both the necessity & impossibility of translation, as Derrida says, in contradiction to the sacred, with its singular & divine origin yet also the self-contradictory logistics of its translational prohibition (a truly sacred text would be self-evident, it would speak for itself without any intermediary or interdiction, it would transcend all need or desire for translation, totalised across all possible languages, being nothing less than "sense" itself, etc.). Comparativism thus arises from a hermeneutic paradox.

[26] In short, through a "teleological" crisis of modernity that defines itself by a certain *disillusionment.*

[27] And which can be situated (somewhat arbitrarily) between the Dreyfus case & the Algerian war of independence, or between Realism & the New Novel. This is something about which much more can obviously be said, but what concerns us here is...

[28] Or as Jacques Lacan punned in his seminar on James Joyce: *père-version.* Which is to say, of *translation... to the father-of-the-logos.* Which is to say, in its Platonic allegorical form, reason. Babel is inverted: the One isn't that which "falls" but which seeks to "rectify" (to "resurrect") in its own image. The "I" that emerges from this resurrection – & *Makbara* ironically refers to those parts of cemeteries used for nocturnal assignations – is a "figure" that doesn't resolve into an "identity": the subject remains in a state of linguistic-ontological perversion.

formed "at will": a dissolution & disillusionment which is that of the text itself & not a simple mimēsis.[29]

The text does not describe but *inscribes* the "polymorphous perversity" (Freud) of a body, a corpus, that is *constitutively heterogeneous*,[30] traversed by such a multiplicity of styles, genres, languages as to be the very contrary of a "utilitarian prose" of eugenic-statist purism.[31] Because if Darwish & Goytisolo's writing *knows* anything about the institution of literature it is that power, no matter how much it turns a blind eye, desires nothing more – & this, perhaps, is the true meaning of its "perversion" – than to *incorporate* its others, to *travesty* all those aberrant textual bodies that would otherwise refuse it: to suborn under the pretext of dignifying, as a "literature of others" if not of "otherness" itself – an otherness which henceforth is compelled to whisper the prose of *its othering*, doubly alienated, doubly prophylactised, so that its barbarous syllables may thenceforth be pronounced without calling down a state of catastrophe, without sacrilegious effect, or anything more insurrectionary than a Mona Lisa smile.

Agadir, February 2023

---

[29] Even as a mimēsis of the insufficiency of power.

[30] It is a corpus that by its nature is always already "other" & calls the very existence of a singular "culture" into question. Whether it does so in the name of its own revulsion, perversity, exclusion, defeatedness, criminality – or as a rejection of these pejoratives – is moot.

[31] "I have always advocated: adding, adding & adding cultures & languages instead of literally eliminating them in the name of a pure identity." Juan Goytisolo with Maria-Àngels Roque, "Interview with Juan Goytisolo," *Quaderns de la Mediterrània* (9 August 2010): https://www.iemed.org/wp-content/uploads/2010/08/Interview-with-Juan-Goytisolo.pdf

2. LITERATURE | THEORY | IDEOLOGY

The reason Milton wrote in fetters when he wrote of Angels & God,
& at liberty when he wrote of Devils & Hell, is because he was a true
Poet & of the Devil's party without knowing it.
>
> (William Blake, *The Marriage of Heaven & Hell*)

Theory begins in action, in a direct engagement!
If, as von Moltke once said, no plan survives first contact with the
enemy, it is precisely at such a *point of contact* – between ideology
& literature – that theory is born. This is not to attribute any kind
of privileged situation to theory, rather the contrary: the encounter
that here initiates itself is the mark of a hegemonic regime asserting
its "right" against an *other* from which every positive status has
been stripped. Theory begins in humiliation. Yet the assertions of
power give rise, despite themselves, to perturbatory effects: either
power, in order to "totalise itself," puts its very meaning at stake, in
a "proof of arms," or risks being a sham. Belonging to a theatre of
ideology costumed as "action," such assertions are a sham in any
case. Power is always a matter of fact; of a prevalence of a system of
meaning. Stripped of the possibility to *mean*, its other ought not to
exist: a contradiction, a paradox. Yet this encounter with the enemy
is not an encounter with a mere "antithesis," one among others, to
be sublimated within an irresistible dialectic, but an encounter with
the *antithetical itself*. To take von Moltke's maxim further: if the
masterplan falters at first contact, this is because its principal *raison*

d'être is to represent what it already knows, since it alone affirms the sovereign domain of meaning & retains its unique prestige only so far as the true "enemy" remains excluded from the field. The task of all hegemonic regimes is thus, in effect, to *become* the enemy, to – as it were – usurp the enemy's place, or rather non-place: to re-inscribe the "figure" of the antithetical *within* its own dialectical schema – such that the faltering-on-first-contact is recast as nothing more than an etiquette of the ritual of sublimation. Such etiquettes are the very foundation of ideological "truth," inevitably eliding with an ideology *of* truth. That a political "fiction" supported by force should demand a monopoly over the field of meaning is perhaps trivial. That it should do so by the suppression of "fiction as such," is worthy of consideration. This, of course, has been the fundamental alignment of reason in western thought since at least Plato, polarised between ideologies of truth, on the one side, & literature on the other. Theory, of more recent provenance, emerges from a deconstruction of this classical schema & the entire edifice of reason built upon it. It begins with questions about the "point of (non) contact" between ideology & its other. It begins with a question about the "literariness" of this discourse of reason & the "rhetorical" nature of its self-address. We have every reason to suppose, then, that this particular constellation of terms – literature, theory, ideology – is of an order other than the purely "arbitrary." In constellation, these terms point to something like a *critical condition* of thought: an emergence, a crisis. This constellation resembles something like a Borromean knot. Just as the Platonic schema describes, not an ideological symptom (one among others), but a universal *symptomatology*, so the Lacanian triad comprising the Borromean knot – real, symbolic, imaginary – is topologically arranged in such a fashion that, while none directly intersect, nor can any *one* be separated without the others also separating.[1] This knot comprises the (w)hole of the subject, just as the constellation literature-theory-ideology might be said to comprise the (w)hole of the semantic field in all its paradox. To paraphrase Foucault, perhaps one day this constellation *will be seen as decisive for meaning in general as the experience of contradiction was for dialectical thought:*

---

[1] See Jacques Lacan, *Seminar XXII: RSI, 1974-5*: nosubject.com/Seminar_XXII

but in spite of so many auguries to this effect, the language in which this constellation will find its space & the illumination of its being lies almost entirely in the future.[2]

"Why then does literature think more than philosophy?"[3]

An immediately combative tone, the beginning of a polemic: Why literature more than philosophy? Why thinking? To whom, literature or philosophy, does the greater burden of thought – of the work & science of thinking – in fact belong? Why should this assertion be in any way controversial, scandalous, newsworthy? Stated as fact, how are we supposed to think about this sentence, in which certain proprietary claims over thought are at the very least implied, while self-consciously bearing the weight of the impropriety of doing so? Consider this proposition: that the name of this impropriety is *theory*. In *Marges de la philosophie*, Derrida raises the question of the proximity of writing & literature to the solicitations of a certain *theoria* in the deconstruction of western metaphysics (a synonymous expression for *the ideology of mimēsis*). *Mimēsis* is more than merely the shadow under the Platonic lamp, the duplicitous companion to the history of philosophy's self-privileging as discourse-of-reason. (The preceding sentence is pleonastic only if we accept the self-evidence of the equation between philosophy & reason "in the first place," an equation whose derivation *post-hoc prompter-hoc* depends upon a détournement of its own mimetic foundation.) Yet this deconstruction is not a simple inversion of terms & their relations, producing a general negation, as in Rancière: "The collapse of the representational paradigm means not only the collapse of a hierarchical system of address; it means the collapse of the whole regime of meaning."[4] To do so would fold "theory" itself back into a representational hierarchy & establish a new "regime of meaning" in the form, e.g., of a negative dialectics. Derrida:

[2] Cf Michel Foucault, *Language, Counter-Memory, Practice*, trans. Donald F. Brouchard & Sherry Simon (Ithaca: Cornell University Press, 1977) 33.

[3] Philippe Sollers, interviewed by Mehdi Belhaj Kacem, "What is the Meaning of the Avant-Garde's Death?" *Diaphanes* 6/7 (11 June 2019), rpr: my-blackout. com/2019/12/20/mehdi-belhaj-kacem-philippe-sollers-what-is-the-meaning-of-the-avant-gardes-death/

[4] Jacques Rancière, "The Politics of Literature" (2003), trans. Steven Corcoran, *Dissensus* (London: Continuum, 2010) 159.

"Everything in talk about metaphor which comes through the sign *eidos*, with the whole system attached to this word, is articulated on the analogy between *our* looking & sensible looking, between the intelligible & the visible sun. The truth of the being that is present is fixed by passing through a detour of tropes in this system… Philosophy, as a theory of metaphor, will first have been a metaphor of theory."[5] Theory's impropriety is thus, in Greg Ulmer's phrasing, to set "Plato's audacity against Platonism."[6] For Derrida, this then entails the demand that "one must simultaneously, by means of rigorous conceptual analyses, philosophically *intractable*, & by the inscription of marks which no longer belong to philosophic space, not even to the neighbourhood of its other, displace the framing, by philosophy, of its own type. Write in another way."[7]

Ideology is (any) system of meaning

The assumption has always been that a system, definitionally, must operate & that in operating must therefore be coherent: that functionality equates to rationality. Yet there is nothing to guarantee this assumption, nothing that underwrites the synonymous relation between "system" & "reason," let alone "system of meaning" & "the meaning of reason." What if the *truth* of such a relation, however, were vested not in its coherence but in the paradox immanent to its terms? If a system can be described algorithmically, as a series of ramifications, where is the line to be drawn between the apparent self-evidence of its *meaning* & the self-assertion of its structural *dogma*? If the Platonic dialectic describes the rudiments of a hermeneutic system, what function does irony serve within it? (The irony, for example, of a philosophical treatise written in the form of a dramatic dialogue – crammed with a veritable odyssey of digressions, allusions, analogies, myths, parables, proxies, fables, symbolism, affect, stylistic flourish, sleight of hand, verbal seduction – essaying a thesis on the priority of interrogative speech to truth & a denunciation of the mimetic arts in general & writing

[5] Jacques Derrida, "White Mythology," *Margins of Philosophy*, trans. Alan Bass (Chicago: University of Chicago Press, 1982) 55-6.
[6] Gregory L. Ulmer, "Theoria," *Applied Grammatology* (Baltimore: Johns Hopkins University Press, 1985) 33.
[7] Derrida, "Tympan," *Margins of Philosophy*, xx.

in particular?) What "resemblance" ought to be found between Plato's philosophical system & the algorithmic irrationalism of Marcel Duchamp's desiring machine ("La mariée mise à nu par ses célibataires, même"), or Gustav Metzger & Jean Tingueley's autodestructive machines? These questions tend in a particular direction: what if all the literary embellishments of Plato's theatrical prose demonstrate the contrary of what is conventionally assumed to be the major distinction between the ideology of *mimēsis* as articulated in the *Dialogues* & that propounded by Aristotle in the *Poetics*? A *mimēsis* bound not to the meaning of truth, but to the production of affect through its supposed apprehension: the truth in pointing, as Derrida puns, being nothing but a *performance* of the truth in painting (& is the persona of "Socrates" not the greatest painter who never lifted a brush?).[8] In other words, what if a certain irony is not the exception to the Platonic system but its general register, not a vehicle employed for rhetorical effect but the foundation of its thought? If the discourse of philosophy no longer represents here the disciplining of the rhetorical figure *per se* but only a simulation of such – a theatrics of reason's dominion over *poiēsis* – then is theory not already implied in the apprehension *(theoria)* of such apparently self-subverting operations? That is to say, as something *like* a "literary" consciousness sublimated within the assertions of philosophical truth & in fact inscribing them – an inscription whose evidence appears nowhere more insistently than in the oft' repeated claim of reason's power *over* writing.

The question of writing puts at stake the meaning of humanity

Insofar as it is a question posed to a certain ideology of reason, of homo *sapiens*. In other words, of a *humanism* which lays claim to the narrative of truth's unveiling. In other words, of history. Yet it is only by virtue of this "putting at stake" that the inscription of a history of reason, or history *as* reason, is brought into a relation of truth in the first place (or, as Karl Popper would have it, of *falsifiability*). This apparent paradox is not given a chance to evolve in Plato, who is content to pose reason in opposition to myth, augury, poetics & the

---

[8] See Jacques Derrida, *The Truth in Painting*, trans. Geoffrey Bennington & Ian McLeod (Chicago: Chicago University Press, 1987).

essential non-being of writing simply in order to assert its priority.[9] How then is the address of this non-being to reason one that is able to put humanity at stake? When Sartre suggests that "one of the chief motives of artistic creation is certainly the need of feeling that we are essential *in* relation to the world"[10] – that humanity is essentially *a relation* to the world (which is not itself transcendental but whose being, in effect, is produced by a certain consciousness of writing) – it is with the question in mind of "whether it is not in the name of this very choice of writing that the self-commitment of writers must be required"?[11] This turn towards writing implies a responsibility that speaks in its own name: the arbitrary is remotivated in the dream of essence, to *signify* more than itself. But it isn't that Sartreanism is merely inverse Platonism, in which a committed consciousness assumes the place of *eidos*, whose actions the world is given to reflect. Where for Plato every *other* is effectively a mirror held up to dialectic, for Sartre it is the other that inscribes the possibility of dialectical thought itself – which is to say, of a true choice. To choose truth is to be "committed," an action whose agency is *writing itself*: the writer is committed by virtue of the choice that writing (re)presents. In the *Phaedrus*, it might just as easily be said that Socrates (he who does not write), machinates against the speechwriting of Lysias because – in order to seduce his comely interlocutor (Phaedrus) away from Lysias' influence – Socrates himself must *usurp the position of writing*. This subsumption of the furtively desired object mirrors the anecdote Socrates relates about the Egyptian scribe-god, in which the *case for writing* is presented & judged *in the absence of testimony on its own behalf* by powers

9 "Memory & truth cannot be separated. The movement of *alētheia* is a deployment of *mnēmē* through & through. [...] The power of *lēthē* simultaneously increases the domain of death, of nontruth, of nonknowledge. This is why writing, at least insofar as it sows "forgetfulness in the soul," turns us towards the inanimate & towards nonknowledge. But it cannot be said that its essence simply & *presently* confounds it with death or nontruth. For writing *has* no essence or value of its own, whether positive or negative. It plays within the simulacrum. It is in its type the mime of memory, of knowledge, of truth, etc." Jacques Derrida, "Plato's Pharmacy," *Dissemination*, trans. Barbara Johnson (Baltimore: Johns Hopkins University Press, 1981) 105.
10 Jean-Paul Sartre, "What is Literature?" [1948], *What is Literature & Other Essays* (London: Methuen, 1950) 27 – emphasis added.
11 Sartre, "What is Literature?" 26.

to whom it is (in light of a *de facto* illiteracy) *unknowable.* While the dialogue appears to concern itself with a reasoned assessment of writing's various deficiencies, it is in fact characterised by hysteria: an hysteria arising from the *threat represented to power by any form of self-sufficiency* & the mirroring desire for *its total (re)possession.*

"There is no art except for & by others"[12]

If, as Sartre argues, "the work of art does not have an end,"[13] this is not because it *is* an end (Kant), or that in it the affordances of *technē* become dialectically entangled with a *poiēses* by which this species of work (*ergon*) is opened to infinitudes. Nor does it simply imply an "autonomous" detachment from teleology, a non-purposiveness or non-subjection to a predetermined design. Rather, it is an assertion that the "work of art" (writing) always already belongs to the future – if by "future" what is meant is a particular otherness to the ideology of *presence* & of history as reason. Sartre may be correct in his belief that the "work of art is a value because it is an appeal"[14] – that is to say, a call or even a calling, *in the suspension of any addressee* or else to the abstraction of a *yet to come.* (It is precisely this that, in the figure of writing, Plato finds so alarming: not the implied patricide by the *logos* capable of autonomous action, but the suspension of reason as universal teleology.) This appeal evokes what Derrida terms destinerrance[15] – both a suspension of address & its generalisation – wherein the signifier is "no longer" bound *to respond* to or for its supposed signified, etc., but to & for a generalised field of *différance.* There remains the suspicion, however, that this will have been the case all along & that only mimetic ideology ever caused it to have the appearance of being otherwise. What would it mean, then, under such conditions, to state, as Sartre does, that "to write is to disclose the world,"[16] unless by "disclosure" what is connoted is the bringing into view of a certain *impossibility* – that is to say, a rupture in the system of reason itself? It may be that it was never really a question of who, or even what, *writes* – rather, & despite Foucault's

[12] Sartre, "What is Literature?" 29.
[13] Sartre, "What is Literature?" 32.
[14] Sartre, "What is Literature?" 34.
[15] Jacques Derrida, "No Apocalypse, Not Now," trans Catherine Porter & Philip Lewis. *Diacritics* 14.2 (1984): 29-30.
[16] Sartre, "What is Literature?" 37.

apparent objections,[17] the question of radical *intransitivity*,[18] one that stems equally from a *subjectlessness*. While the implications of Sartre's argument introduce a contradiction between the egoic notion of the committed artist, on the one hand, & an autopoetic inscription of world-consciousness, on the other, this contradiction is not resolved simply by asserting, as Foucault does, "the 'ideological' status of the author."[19] Between ideological agency & its other(s), there is no simple relation: the question – what *is* non-ideological agency? – cannot, within such an epistemology, yield a meaningful response. Likewise, just as the myth of Homer is not the antagonist of reason that Plato more than implies in his polemic on the *ideal polis*, but rather a foil, an "ideological construct," so too the myth of the author, which, even as it is supposedly abolished, is here re-valorised in a somewhat *panoptical* relation to all those terms constellated around it (from work to text, etc.). This authorial Götterdämmerung is nothing if not ambivalent. While it isn't enough, as Foucault says, "to repeat the empty affirmation that the author has disappeared,"[20] nor is it sufficient to observe that "the author is not an indefinite source of significations which fill a work; the author does not precede the works; he is a functional principle by which, in our culture, one limits, excludes & chooses; in short by which one impedes the free circulation, the free manipulation, the free composition, decomposition & recomposition of fiction."[21] Apart from its neoliberal overtones, this argument remains centred around a paranoiac conception of a *deus ex machina* secretly operating behind the mask of an ideological construct in order to impede the freedom of a significatory system that exists *because* it is a fiction (a fiction within a fiction). What is this "one" if not *ideology itself*, given the status of a distributed panoptical agency? Is it the case that *ideology as such* could ever be susceptible in this way to an inverted representation, even if only as the spectre of a

---

[17] See Michel Foucault, "What is an Author?" [1963], *The Foucault Reader*, ed. Paul Rabinow (London: Penguin, 1984).
[18] See Roland Barthes, "To Write: An Intransitive Verb?" *The Rustle of Language*, trans. Richard Howard (Berkeley; University of California Press, 1986) 11-21.
[19] Foucault, "What is an Author?" 113.
[20] Foucault, "What is an Author?" 103.
[21] Foucault, "What is an Author?" 113.

fear (whose?) of "the proliferation of meaning?"[22] If, when Sartre says that "the world is my task," he means *the task of writing*, it is also to writing that Foucault implicitly assigns responsibility for that ideological figure of the author who, in this cryptomimetic melodrama, is concocted to guard against "the great peril, the great danger with which fiction threatens our world."[23] But where for Sartre "the world appears as the horizon of our situation"[24] (which is to say, "as the infinite space that separates humanity from itself, as the synthetic totality of the given, as the undifferentiated whole of obstacles & impediments, but never as a demand addressed to our freedoms"), for Foucault the problem begins with an inverse phenomenology, as a consciousness devolving from situatedness (i.e. the figure of the author mirrors a subject). A consciousness produced not as dialectic, but (though it is never named as such) as *autopoiēsis*. The problem remains one of *figuration*, the reduction of an autonomous field of inscriptive potential to a humanist metaphorics of authoritarianism, on the one hand, & freedom on the other; from a general signifying condition to a conspiracy.

The portrait of a Mona Lisa smile

A hegemonic conception of history (is there any other?) reduces to the view that there is only ever one "universal" narrative: that of domination & its attendant consciousness. The fact remains that, for Plato, *mimēsis isn't primarily a regime for the valorisation of "truth,"* but of authority over the distribution of meaning. That is to say, the valorisation of power. In Plato, the author is not *committed*, since the responsibility born by the author is *a priori* that of authority itself: dialectic is not critique; the work of art is never conceived as either aesthetically or politically autonomous, yet neither is the author, who remains subject to (contracted to) the judgement of "truth." In this way, the locus of every "dialogue" is effectively fixed in advance, *irrespective of its form*. But this locus is barely more than an *assertion* of power, one that demands (pre-empts) at every moment the assent of discourse itself. The motto of this regime of philosophic authoritarianism might just as well

<hr>

[22] Foucault, "What is an Author?" 120.
[23] Foucault, "What is an Author?" 115.
[24] Sartre, "What is Literature?" 36.

be, then: *vérité et mon droit*. Beneath the dialectical subtleties of its various manoeuvres of recuperation, the philosophical project inaugurated by Plato ultimately amounts to a confidence game. Just as the analogy of the cave presented in *The Republic* is grounded in little more than the *assertions* of its narrator (the mimetic prison, the light of truth), so too its general hermeneutic devolves upon the insertion of metanarratological devices by which the action of having arrived at a given of truth is *insisted upon* (the conclusion of *The Sophist* is perhaps the most conspicuous occurrences). This reliance upon a literary *deus ex machina* not only exposes certain limits to (or contradictions within) the philosophical project as discourse-of-truth, but situates these very limits (which it actively sublimates) as in fact its principal consideration. Philosophy's authority over these limits henceforth equates to a substantiation of its truth. In this respect Ulmer contends that "philosophy is that discourse which has taken as its object its own limit. It appropriates the concept of the limit & believes that it can dominate its own margin & think its other."[25] In this, philosophy, like capital in Marx's critique, is marked equally by "internal contradictions" & a magical ability to incorporate all "external" forms of negation. Nothing about this should be surprising, since what is at stake is a recursive system, a dialectics *of dialectics*. The "truth" to which this recursive system refers is always already an operation of metaphor, of proxification as *discourse-of-truth*, which is to say, "philosophy." The two do not simply elide: they produce one another, by a circuit of constant ramification, a feedback loop, a "universal" algorithm. Not only does this predetermine the unique access Platonism is able to lay claim to with regard to this truth, but it establishes the basis for the entire future of that project referred to as Western metaphysics. That it does so by affirming *its own historical dimension* is in no way paradoxical (even if, as Rancière argues, it is *literature* that has the power to convert things into signs of history, since philosophy, here, *already is literature*). In this way, truth, as Ulmer observes, is not simply narrated by philosophy; it itself is attributed "a history," & this history affords it the privilege of incorporating all of the contradictory meanings signed in its name, just as science,

[25] Ulmer, "Theoria," 30-31.

too, is afforded the means to "appropriate all of its revolutions because of the transcendental, idealising function of dialectical thinking."[26] (The subsequent *institutionalisation* of the concept of "universal revolution" – which Harvey Wheeler identified with the cyberneticisation of Western systems of politico-economic communication & control after WW2 – affirms this key element of Platonic ideology.[27]) This twofold historical placement – truth as both *subject* of history & its *teleology* – has the ironic consequence of entangling truth in the very mythos from which Plato had apparently redeemed it by exiling poetics from the ideal philosophical polis. Such a truth, *like literature* – being thus revealed to be "a rationale equal to history"[28] – describes a hermeneutic circle of which it itself is the supposed object, while the exclusory regime affected in its name becomes the most conspicuous sign of the fact that there are *others* (other "rationales") that do not correspond to the Platonic phantasm of "the other in a hierarchically organised relationship."[29]

Philosophy begins from the position
of being on the side of history

Philosophy (reason) is that sign placed upon the "amorphous body" of myth & which thereafter regulates its poetic under the law of genre. This is the narrative Plato assigns to what he casts as the principal antagonists of philosophy: writing & poetry, hereafter bound in a dialectics of subjection. The scenario is well known: poetry, writing, on the side of untruth, are exiled from the *polis*, yet given leave to plead in their defence before the tribunal of reason, but only in the authorised language of philosophic prose (poetry itself, writing itself, must not "speak").[30] Picture a regime of Kafkaesque gatekeepers, principle among them a frustrated playwright passing off his manuscripts as philosophical treatises,

---

[26] Ulmer, "Theoria," 33.

[27] Harvey Wheeler, *Democracy in a Revolutionary Era* (Santa Barbara: The Centre for the Study of Democratic Institutions, 1968) 14.

[28] Hélène Cixous, "Sorties," *The Newly Born Woman*, trans. B. Wing (Minneapolis: University of Minnesota Press, 1986) 66.

[29] Cixous, "Sorties," 70.

[30] Just as theory will be repeatedly subjected to the judgement of a certain *academic style*, one that will simultaneously attempt to recuperate it as an exemplary form of quasi-literary artefact while erecting a *discipline* around it.

ventriloquised in the name of a notorious enemy of the state. These ironies run deep, fuelling an attitude of "legitimate concerns" that ought to appear as self-satire & yet inaugurate what may be described as an hysterical contagion, propagated in reaction to the plague of *mimēsis*, fiction, untruth, myth & other "imaginary" infections of the rational mind. Are poetry, writing, here merely the scapegoats of an unrestrained paranoia or a cynical powerplay? But already this question has us chasing shadows. It seems a cliché readymade: Plato, failed dramatic poet, resentful of the universal acclaim of Homer inverted in the figure of Socrates, while opportunistically exploiting the dead man's legacy – perhaps. (It's tempting to consider the entire Platonic oeuvre as a desire to write Socrates *in advance*, to script His Master's Voice as a movement of Oedipal *jouissance* open to perpetual repetition, each "dialogue" re-inscribing, with variations, this primal scene).[31] Internecine warfare is often the most ruthless, the most brutal. What else would it look like were one idea of literature to wage war against its other(s), elevated in degrees of consequence to a drama of the state & even, say, the founding precepts of "civilisation," if not of the species as a whole? Hardly preposterous when we consider that the first known systems of graphic signs (including knots, constellations, architectures, burial arrangements) correspond to the abstraction of ritual, the emergence of bureaucracies, denominations of exchange, the extension of power over remote territories & the formalisation of "objective," "universal" history. Nor when we consider that many of the oldest examples of *writing* represent the codification of laws, themselves often composed in *poetic form*. Ought we not consider Platonism, then, as precisely a repetition-rehearsal of this primal scene – the dialectical "mirror

[31] What is Socrates but a *textual figure*, composed of irony, catachresis, transgression? The peripatetic philosopher in whom truth is always centred. He who drinks but remains sober. He who does not write, etc. A tireless busybody, corrupter of the youth, who "permits himself" to stray outside the walls of the *polis*, into areas hostile to the discourse of reason, in order to seduce the impressionable, overly-credulous, (or merely bored?) Phaedrus away from the *false arts.* Socrates: the *logos* that disguises itself & goes abroad *in order to arrive at* (return to) *its true destination, the destination of truth* (the republic of reason). Socrates: the *logos* of reason itself? Whose itinerary, guided by an avowed pursuit of truth, resembles nothing so much as a literary occasion, at worst an alibi, for his puppet-master to put reason itself on stage & (quelle idée!) *put words in its mouth.*

stage" of a primordial literacy henceforth bound in perpetual, quasi-evolutionary struggle between *its* institutional & fugitive forms – its Babelisation?

Is truth a situation "ceded," like a poisoned pawn, to reason by its other(s)?

"Literature," Deleuze writes, "is delirium," & "all delirium is world historical."[32] Alluding to Goya, Derrida similarly evokes the expression "slumber of reason," which is a "slumber that engenders monsters & then puts them to sleep… this slumber must be effectively traversed so that awakening will not be a ruse of dream." Literature (writing) is *delirious* only insofar as it itself is doubled by *a ruse of reason*. "The slumber of reason is not, perhaps, reason put to sleep," Derrida argues, "but slumber in the form of reason."[33] When Barthes proposes that "literature is a *mathēsis*, an order, a system, a structured field of knowledge,"[34] it is worth considering that these terms are likewise subjected to a *détournement*: firstly, that the "ruse of reason" is orientated by the claim that it is *the opposite of literature.* The totalising movement of its discourse thus falls into contingency: that philosophy is *contingent* upon literature; that reason itself is the monster engendered by an insurrectionary dream of writing (at least as Plato imagines it in the *Phaedrus*). Literature is not an eruption on the margins of reason, but the entire terrain reason seeks to occupy (while retaining for itself, here & there, reserves of domesticated poignancy: lyric reveries that may recall Socrates' monologue on love, which is really just philosophy serenading itself in drag). When Barthes speaks, apropos of Severo Sarduy's *Cobra* & *Maitreya*,[35] of *the pleasure of the text* he is not exclusively referring to those exotic language effects of socalled avantgarde anti-literature, but to the convulsions of that same discourse of reason against which avantgardism is conventionally opposed:

[32] Gilles Deleuze, "Literature & Life," *Essays Critical & Clinical*, trans. D.W. Smith & M.A. Greco (Minneapolis: University of Minnesota Press, 1997) 2.
[33] Jacques Derrida, "From Restricted to General Economy: An Hegelianism without Reserve," *Writing & Difference*, trans Alan Bass (London: Routledge, 1978) 252.
[34] Roland Barthes, *Roland Barthes*, trans. Richard Howard (Berkeley: University of California Press, 1977) 118.
[35] Roland Barthes, *The Pleasure of the Text*, trans. Richard Miller (New York: Hill & Wang, 1975).

a discourse that, obsessed as it is with policing its categories, still cannot imagine its own *finitude*, even as it claims to establish, each time, the meaning of its truth as if *once & for all*. Reason continuously invents (fictionalises) other futures for itself, through the *pleasure of contradiction*, the *eroticism of dialectics*. It is forever transgendering itself even as it professes the one true "phallogocentric" faith. (Not for nothing does Derrida deconstruct Hegel via a montage of Genet.[36]) Such ambiguities are not the exception: divergence, duplicity, ambivalence – none of the terms under discussion here belongs to a singular genealogy, gender or genre.

The field of "literature" isn't a fait accompli

If literature assumes the form of something that announces itself in advance, it does so by presenting the indeterminacy of its own limits. Rancière, following Foucault, insists on the modernity of the concept of literature: a *modo* nevertheless immanent to its antiquity (its "nascent state"[37]). It isn't enough for the institution of literature to be bound to a certain (restricted) history *of* writing, it must define the very *discontinuity* of that history, itself a history of discontinuities (including the socalled *tradition of the new*?[38]). Literature's "modernity," then, like the attendant phenomenon of avant-gardism, would amount to both a prefiguring of literature's institutional closure, which nevertheless remains provisional (orientated by the movement of *institutionalisation*: that is to say, openness to expropriation of its other[s]) & an eruptive negation. In Plato's system of exclusions & judicial co-option (show trials, in effect), this movement always presents itself as one that *supervenes*[39] in history & in this respect *authors* it. What then comes to present itself as a counter-discourse, in the revolutionary form of an avant-garde, is likewise immanent to this *movement of history*: its autonomous appearance being effectively bound – in advance – within a dialectics that affects the sole claim to self-

[36] See Jacques Derrida, *Glas*, trans. J.P. Leavey & Richard Rand (Nebraska: University of Nebraska Press, 1990).
[37] See Jean-François Lyotard, *The Postmodern Condition: A Report on Knowledge*, trans. Geoff Bennington & Brian Massumi (Manchester: Manchester University Press, 1991) 81.
[38] See Harold Rosenberg, *The Tradition of the New* (New York: DaCapo, 1960).
[39] Strategically or tactically.

sufficiency (as such). Several conflicting provenances of literature emerge from this schema to foreshadow the problem of a certain *return of history* as writing & of writing *as theory*, yet the problem lies not in reconciling these differing genealogies, but in drawing out the *system of differences* that mimes their production "in the first place." This generalised dialectic is a genre machine. But its genres, its categories, are themselves tropic, discursive effects; its operations construe a *techno-poetics*. To speak of the situation of "literature" here is, therefore, to speak both of *autonomy* & of the relation (or non-relation) between politics & ideology. That is to say, of the double-bind of "writing power."[40] Under the guise of a *genre of genres*, the dialectical theatre inscribes itself & is inscribed by the mechanical genius of a power that is nothing if not ambivalent. Its teleology is a perpetuum mobile. It bears the inscrutable mark of automatic revolution. Like a resultant infinity it presents both as trivial & as threatening to the entire edifice of the system of meaning.[41] If, as Aurelius insists, actions are the only facts, then this power is ultimately indecisive, yet it is absolutely determinate.

"What is democracy if not the equal ability to be democrat, anti-democrat or indifferent to both democracy & anti-democracy?"[42] There is a moment in the Second Manifesto of Surrealism (1929) when André Breton declares that the "simplest surrealist act" would be to go down into the street, pistol in hand, & fire randomly into the crowd.[43] This statement is many things & has provoked many responses, yet the outrage it sometimes occasioned often elides the contemporary patriotic mythos that continued to enshroud WW1 & obscure its horrors (symptomatic of a more general tendency that, even after the revelation of Nazi deathcamps in WW2, was barely disrupted until the Vietnam War & the radicalisation of the socalled counterculture, though likewise with reactionary effect). Taken as a metaphor of the avantgarde in general, in what contrast does this "simplest surrealist act" present the revolt of art, or

---

[40] See Jacques Derrida, "Scribble (writing-power)," trans. Cary Plotkin, *Yale French Studies* 58 (1979): 117-147.
[41] A "writing degree zero" also implies infinities.
[42] Rancière, "The Politics of Literature," 155.
[43] André Breton, *Manifestoes of Surrealism*, trans. Richard Seaver (Ann Arbor: University of Michigan Press, 1969).

socalled anti-art, to the apparatus of the corporate-state? By most estimates, WW1 produced some 40 million casualties. Its senseless terror & destruction bore unprecedented social consequences. The institutional culture of the time was entirely inadequate to articulate any of this, beyond restatements of existing aesthetic forms in the service of pathos. But the outrage of Breton's pronouncement has nothing to do with mathematics or pathos & everything to do with that void concealed within a certain attitude of *ambivalence*, an effect the surrealists recognised in Gide's celebration of *l'acte gratuit*.[44] To speak *literally* of 40 million senseless casualties, is to evoke a cataclysm of random acts, the operations of a mechanical universe revealed to be naked of a humanly-meaningful teleology. To be one individual firing, however randomly, into a crowd is, on the contrary, to present what is in effect an insurmountable *moral* problem: here, the gesture itself *bears responsibilities*, even if its authorship, & the consequences it in turn authors, are said to be arbitrary, the apparently perverse (unconscious, reflexive) impulses of an indiscriminate agent of the will-to-power. It is not simply that a belief in certain causalities is disturbed more by the one than the other. The question, vested as it is in a highly ambiguous metaphor (surrealism itself), has to do with the relation between a regime of power that is globally manifest in the very unironic disposal of mass violence, & a power whose "forms" are not attempts at a *mimēsis* but the contrary: "forms" of sabotage, parody, critique – the *grotesquerie* of an ideo-political world denied the solace of aestheticisation ("We have nothing to do with literature... We are specialists in Revolt"[45]). And what, then, of an aesthetics that comes armed against precisely such a solace? The "violence" not of an avantgardist provocation, but of the systemic ambivalence it arises from: an ambivalence from within the very logic & discourse of meaning, & its subjection in the figure of writing?

[44] See André Gide, *Les Caves du Vatican* (Paris: NRF, 1914).
[45] Bureau of Surrealist Research, "Declaration of 27 January 1925," *Surrealism Against the Current: Tracts & Declarations*, eds. Michael Richardson & Krzysztof Fijalkowski (London: Pluto, 2001) 24.

The inhuman is only the "other side" of humanism

"If art is to be art, it must be politics; if it is to be politics, the monument must speak twice-over: as a résumé of human effort & as a résumé of the power of the inhuman separating the human from itself."[46] Not to be distracted by the *terms* of this formulation, what Rancière draws attention to here is that the first principle is always the *exception.* This isn't a paradox but the foundation of its identity. In the Platonic narrative, poetry is placed before the tribunal of reason under duress: we are to believe that the imposition of *prose* as the language of appeal will lock poetry in a double-bind, just as writing is bound in the advocacy of *speech.* Yet this logos is presented from the outset in the form of a rebus (speech, as metaphor of a communicable eidos, always already implies its detachable "other"; poetics inscribes, in advance as it were, all the rhetorical devices of intellectual persuasion, of the communicability of "truth," etc.). Writing, as Derrida says, *comes before* speech, as the very possibility of an inscription of difference & so on. Is this duress, then, a fiction? At precisely that point in the system of *mimēsis* where paternal authority over the logos is itself placed *under duress* by the threat posed in writing, an inversion takes place. But what does it signify when power declares itself to be in danger? When a certain humanity is called upon in defence of what is, in effect, the apotheosis of the inhuman? (Reason, in Plato, is always on the side of the transcendental.) If we are to speak of the "resistance" of writing, then, this cannot be *in reaction*: the entire Platonic universe comes into view only as a consequence of the fact of writing; its consciousness is born, as it were, of a *missed inscription*, in which it becomes aware – like the Freudian polymorphous perverse – of not coinciding with totality. (Nothing is brought so clearly into focus in the *Dialogues* than the sense of philosophy's belatedness, of its need to demonstrate itself adequate to the task of imitating reason, such that it can even claim *to be* reason, while simultaneously announcing an obligation to defend that claim against competitors & adversaries who, despite its aspiration to omnipotence, it feels compelled to relentlessly defame.) This theatre of infantile authoritarianism, whose acme is

[46] Jacques Rancière, "The Monument & its Confidences; or Deleuze & Art's Capacity for 'Resistance'" (2003), trans. Steven Corcoran, *Dissensus*, 172.

The Republic's micromanaged vision of an "ideal polis," represents the antithesis of a politics: its appeal to reason exceeds the realm of contestable social relations, all of which are to be subject to its rationale. It isn't a matter of imposing one ideology or another, since in the figure of reason what we are purportedly given is the figure of the non-ideological itself, of self-evident Truth, etc. Which is to say, as Althusser was right to insist, *of ideology as such*. This handydandy gaslit dialecticism is the entire Platonic method. *Look*, Plato says in "The Cave," *everything you thought was real is a fake*. And, like Hamlet, he parades a troop of players in front of his audience to show the truth of the matter. "What? Frighted by false fire?" The question is rhetorical, of course: Plato's antagonists are always rendered mute, we're only offered straightmen he can bat Socrates' gags off. As if acquiescing to Plato's terms, Rancière (attributing this thought to Deleuze) discovers the principal role of art, literature, writing, politics to be one of *resistance*: "The resistance of the work," he ventriloquises, "isn't art's way of rescuing politics; it is not art's way of imitating or anticipating politics – it is properly speaking their identity. Art *is* politics."[47] Between these two metaphors – philosophy as reason; art as politics – what is assumed to be taking place?

The judgement of praxis
Historically, the emergence of the avantgarde in the mid-19th century corresponds with a particular constellation of ideas about revolutionary theory, social praxis, autonomy of action & the construction of political consciousness. Into each of these formulations the terms "art" or "aesthetics" entered into a direct correspondence: either by sublimation (the incorporation of revolutionary discourse as a subject of institutional art history) or solicitation (a systematic destabilising of this history). Adopting the function of a vanguard party, the new art affected two parallel tasks: 1. a critique of everything that had come to define the field of culture & *its specific relation to power*; 2. a self-critical *permanent revolution* directed at its own status & procedures within that relation. Since the 1970s a tragic view of avantgardism has determined this project (of working the socalled gap between "art" & "everyday life") to

<hr>

[47] Rancière, "The Monument & its Confidences," 172.

have failed. Peter Bürger, extending a selective line of reasoning from Adorno's *Culture Industry*, has suggested that "the systemic self-criticism of art"[48] not only aligns with what, increasingly after 1968, is an implicitly institutional mechanism of co-option (versus those forms of institutional inertia that had formerly "evolved" only at the height of crisis), but that it fails precisely because it pretends to stand *in opposition* to institutionalisation *as such*. Bürger's version of the tragic view of the avantgarde is often framed as a simple distinction between an historical avantgarde (Futurism, Dada, Surrealism) that performed a *Destruktion* of the social contract between art & morality (the relation of power to the "good") & a post-war neoavantgarde in which these same gestures were merely re-enacted *within* & *for* the institutions of culture, thus serving to reaffirm that contract (even if under varied terms). Some critics of Bürger have argued that this schema is not simply reductive (naïve dialecticism), but that it depends on "exclusively emphasising that the autonomy of art is an ideological value which is a function of the commodity-form," while appealing to a belief in "non-commodity social forms & relations" in order to sustain an *alternative*.[49] While the case of Bürger may simply be one of nostalgia for certain fixed dualisms, a more important consideration arises here. While Marx had already recognised the revolutionary consequences of commodification for what, until the mid-19th century (that is to say, coincident with the emergence of avantgardism), was understood by the terms "capital" & "capitalism," there remained a persistent belief that the "commodity-form" could be understood simply as an *instrument* of capital, even if one capable of affecting its (capitalism's) "internal" transformation beyond any kind of fixed political meaning. It would only be the advent of a theoretical tendency vested in the semiological studies of Ferdinand de Saussure & others (largely bypassing the "critical theory" of the Frankfurt School to which Bürger was indebted) that would bring into view the deep relation between the *arbitrary* character of sign systems in general & the universal characteristics of the commodity-

---

[48] Peter Bürger, *Theory of the Avant-Garde*, trans. Michael Shaw (Minneapolis: University of Minnesota Press, 1984) 20.
[49] Gavin Grindon, "Surrealism, Dada & the Refusal of Work: Autonomy, Activism & Social Participation in the Radical Avant-Garde," *Oxford Art Journal* 34.1 (2011): 82.

form, giving rise to a radical understanding of ideology founded not in a critique of *hierarchies of value* but in the *ambivalence of meaning* that makes them possible.

The deferral of ends & the fantasy of self-supersession

"Politics," Rancière writes, "is first of all a way of framing, among sensory data, a specific sphere of experience. It is a partition of the sensible, of the visible & the sayable, which allows (or does not allow) some specific data to appear; which allows or does not allow some specific subjects to designate them & speak about them."[50] It is a specific intertwining of ways of being, ways of doing & ways of speaking. Politics belongs, in other words, to the domain of logistics – it is always, "first of all," *technē politikē.* What permits this political technology to operate is the inscription *avant la lettre* of a radical commodity-form which Rancière, via the writings of Balzac & Flaubert, characterises by *indifference*. The world of sensory data is presented, by way of a literary framing device, in Balzac's analogy of a bric-a-brac shop, whose jumble of expired commodities has been reduced to *stuff* – the "it" to which the term *commodity* originally attached – like Roquentin's pebble on the beach at Bouville. This *stuff* resembles, insofar as it resembles anything, a "system" of pure entropy, a circulatory dead-end of "mute letters," as Rancière says, that signify only the fact of their indifference (to any given system of value). Yet it is precisely this signifying minimum that permits these mute letters – this *lumpenproletariat* of debased commodities – to be revalorised *as signifiers of political possibility*. But only insofar as it reveals the basis of all symbolic exchange upon a certain *indifference* (& a certain *différance*) "first of all." Not unlike Sartre, the motive force of this revalorisation for Rancière remains the assumption of a subject: a figure in which the "partition of the sensible" (its re-*differentiation*) acquires a cognitive architecture – a political consciousness – amounting to an "idea" of structure. This *thought* would thus assume the appearance of an autonomous action, in which politics ("a way of framing") thinks itself as political subject. It is this reflexivity that Rancière equates to literature, as the distinction between subjective fantasy & the phantasmal world

50 Rancière, "The Politics of Literature," 153.

(the "partition of the sensible"): "The politics of literature thus means that literature as literature is involved in this partition of the visible & sayable, in this intertwining of being, doing & saying that frames a polemical common world."[51] This ontological dream is, for Rancière, the proper domain of an "autonomous" literature that, by virtue of its autonomy, is properly political. (Breton & Trotsky will have formulated a comparable line of argument in their joint 1938 manifesto "Towards a Free Revolutionary Art.") And this autonomy stems from a radical *indifference*: "the 'indifference' of a way of writing & the opposite statements it allows for."[52] This polysemy gives allowance not only of a certain "free play" of signification but of *the idea of opposition as such*. In advance of any political system stands this *polemical precondition* – such that what Rancière calls the political isn't an enunciation of the world so much as its *a priori* alienation by way of its "essential" otherness (its "democratic" character of *equivalence*). The question is not, however, to situate a politics *of* literature, but the political as a mode of inscription, of the indifference/différance of a writing that opens the possibility of a "polemical common world" in the first place. Rancière attempts to resolve this by an appeal to a certain modernity of literature "as such," as "the modern regime of the art of writing," beyond the "opposition between the servitude of *mimēsis* & the autonomy of self-referentiality."[53] Such a literature is marked by "the democratic availability of the 'dead letter'" – or "mute letter" – "the letter that anybody can receive."[54] The possibility of *being in receipt* of such a letter is, in effect, to be a *political subject*. Is not the entire discourse of politics, asks Rancière, not "a plot invented by literature itself?"[55]

Prague, May 2022

[51] Rancière, "The Politics of Literature," 153.
[52] Rancière, "The Politics of Literature," 153.
[53] Rancière, "The Politics of Literature," 155-56.
[54] Rancière, "The Politics of Literature," 158.
[55] Rancière, "The Politics of Literature," 164.

3. CRISIS IN THE TIMEMACHINE

Structures don't go out onto the streets... (Sorbonne graffiti, 1968)

avant-neo-post

There is a tendency in narratives about the avantgarde to devolve into trenchant debate about its revenant failures, its historical discontinuity & its contemporary impossibility. Conspicuously, the locus of much of this debate isn't a material history of the avantgarde itself, but a subjective psychodrama around another supposed "failure," that of 1968 (itself a relay between the "failure" of the wider revolutionary project in Europe after 1917 & of the worldwide antiglobalisation movement at the end of the millennium). In many ways, the supposed *recuperation* of the discourse of the avantgarde has served as a proxy for the disillusionments & resentments of a historical moment it is often itself excluded from, by an act of critical foreclosure that seeks to *terminate* its historical project. In this manner, the tragic view of revolutionary possibility after 1968 is given to reprise the tragic view of aesthetic possibility after Auschwitz, itself a discordant reprise of the Dadaist's *parodic* view of political morality after WW1 & that of Rimbaud et al. after the Paris Commune. At each point something like an End of History has been evoked, in a continual renovation of Hegel's messianism, & in language often attributed to Marx in which it is in the "nature" of history to *repeat*, only with the terms inverted: farce & then tragedy (farce being the temper of the avantgarde; tragedy, that of its critics).

Recuperation, assimilation, institutionalisation: these recurrent motifs point towards a curious phenomenon. The oft' repeated claim of the death or failure of the avantgarde is unable to mask the fact that institutionalisation remains an ongoing – which is to say, *incomplete* – project. In this sense, institutionalisation appears to be marked by a certain insufficiency. While the accelerated cycle of recuperation – to the point of seeming instantaneous in an age of digital media – implies that the *avantgarde function* has itself become increasingly "internalised" to that of the institution, this image of totality remains, despite many apocalyptic claims to the contrary, unable to suture itself, to constitute that unique "autonomy" of an ideal-ego.[1]

Doubtless the omnipotence of the institution – its inexorable tendency to neutralise everything upon which its gaze happens to fall – has been grossly overstated. Its apparent "success" at incorporating various notions of the avantgarde, moreover, are not what they seem: its exhibits, we might easily suspect, are caricatures, a Wunderkammer stuffed with taxidermized corpses, a trophy room. Moreover, these creatures never existed, they were invented in an anatomy theatre, pieced together from the merely recognisable *orts, scraps & fragments* of something incomprehensible to a "science" capable of *no other* interest in them. But it isn't merely that the spectre of the avantgarde haunts the institutions of art capital, rendering these caricatures grotesque, but that an "unassimilable" element persists – not in upsetting the arrangement, but in making it possible.

Crisis doesn't *befall* the system of representation
Let us suppose that avantgardism (a concept that emerges more or less contemporaneously with Hegel's thesis on the end of art) bears within it the assertion that *history (too) has an end* – & that this end of history is expressed through the belief that it can be *precipitated* through a direct assault on a teleological order of fixed hierarchical

---

[1] Are we not always at risk, here, of extending too much credit to a system built on a certain market confidence, whose predominant currency is self-assertion? Does not criticism acquiesce to power the moment it allows institutionalisation to define the comprehension, & thus recuperation, of that which "contradicts it" merely because it says it does? Merely, in other words, by sticking a pricetag on it in place of a target?

(aesthetic & social) values, in order to bring a previously occluded future into being. If the avantgarde emerges or merges with a certain dialectical thought of human consciousness, of the "present of the human mind" enchained to the past & desirous of projecting into the future (emancipation), this is because under conditions of modernity the prospect of a universal consciousness first comes into being *as a constituent of everyday life.* It is in this sense that the avantgarde speaks of aesthetic revolution as a direct relation between art & life, which is to say between *two modes of representation.*

The avantgarde can thus be seen as an assault upon the concept of history *as foreclosure of revolutionary thought*: that is to say, as a history of impossibilities. One of the significations of the term avantgarde, then, is *revolution of history or the demand for the impossible. Insofar as Hegel bequeaths to it the idea that history itself can be thought as a mode of revolution,* then the avantgarde presents itself as *revolution of revolution*. It is for this reason, among others, that the historical ruptures *within* the avantgarde need to be understood in terms not of a self-negation by successive countermovements, but in terms of the seemingly contrary phenomenon of *institutionalisation.*

To paraphrase Kojève, a term is "only" the history of its interpretation – a notion, constitutionally rife with contradiction (history, i.e., not *of* but *as* a sum-total of contradictory "interpretations") which has led to a paradoxical sense of the avantgarde as a tendency to perpetrate acts of insurrection doomed to a negative existence: that avantgardism, by pursuing a *permanent revolution*, nihilistically subverts *the very gesture of a "seizure of power."* Doomed, therefore, to a form of impotent recuperation within the confines of those institutions of art capital against which its subversive force is intended to be directed. This in turn has given rise to a way of thinking that orientates the idea of the avantgarde in a fixed relation to "its object," as a kind of rectifying conscience in a system of social relations in demand of a moral imperative. The avantgarde's failure to supply such rectifications has given rise to a certain "tragic view," by which the various "neo-avantgardes" are perceived as cynically defeatist re-enactments of a false promise (rather than a consciousness, for example, that such rectification is impossible: at a fundamental level, *there is not social relation*). In this narrative, the avantgarde becomes a myth, parallel to that of the political itself, one that is animated solely by its failure.[2] And yet, the recurrent paroxysms of socalled "culture wars" would seem to indicate that the "subversive" power of certain avantgardist ideas in & of art, literature, cinema etc., continues to exert a disproportionate influence[3] – more than capable of incitement to the various hysterias that comprise the status quo – just as, over two millennia past, certain ideas of poetics & writing had done in the work of Plato.

There is no *other* "system of meaning"

In *The Republic*, the translation of poetry into prose, as precondition for the former's advocacy before the tribunal of reason, provides a founding allegory of what institutionalisation entails.

From this, two parallel lines of thought unfold:

The first implies an institution whose structures verge upon the logical rigidity of a psychosis, even if this rigidity takes on the appearance of a dialectics; an openness to incorporating the "other."

---

[2] The "failure" of the avantgarde, which Peter Bürger identifies with its subsequent reiterations & post-effects, was already well in evidence in its socalled "historical" phase. We see the particular significance of Prague Dada in the "failure" of Dada globally not because of its obscurity or suppression, but because, as Hausmann noted, it was the site, in the early 1920s, of Dada's greatest "success": that is to say, of its total assimilation as bourgeois entertainment. The virulent Dadaism of John Heartfield's Prague-period photomontages, produced in the service of antifascist critique, were likewise neutralised in their subversive force by an analogous populism. The same would occur with the advent of the Museum of Modern Art & the assimilation of the avantgarde within the spectacle of institutional art history, now defined by showcasing "movements": modern art, it proposed, may be *temperamental*, but its temperamentality is still comprehensible within a broadly dialectical schema in which the foundation of continuity is discontinuity. What Rosenberg later termed the *tradition of the new*.

[3] This disproportion expresses itself in the relation of force to farce – a common feature across an otherwise heterogeneous field. Even the most straightfaced rendering of Marinetti's Futurist Manifesto cannot conceal the deeply farcical character of its bombast – a farce that isn't merely for performative effect, but goes to the core of the inability of a regime of signifying power to comprehend & articulate that which is alien to it. The Futurist Manifesto is a masterclass in mixed metaphor – of organicism rent by an inchoate technopoetics: its magisterial tones *underwhelm* the language in which they are expressed & which in turn they fatally sabotage. Tzara's Dada manifesto deconstructs the language & logic of the manifesto itself by a contrary strategy: it is nothing if not exemplary of a certain rationalism. As Foucault came later to demonstrate: reason includes the irrational *within* its own logic: Plato's dichotomy of exclusion, isolation & disempowerment of poetry by way of the philosophic institution of syllogistic prose amounts to fiction.

The second implies an "other" that is always already negated in advance, as poetry is negated in the Platonic schema & translated into the prose of reason: in effect, holding up a mirror to the power of its "subversion of subversion."[4]

In these acts of enclosure of the cultural field, the avantgarde serves as an ideal trophy. So when it is said that the avantgarde is anti-institutional, what does this mean?

Jacques Lacan, referring to the paranoid ego of civilisation (culture), presents a counter-intuitive understanding of "true freedom" as stemming not from an overthrowing of institutions & a seizure of power, but from a *consciousness* of not being free at all. The Surrealist revolution, for example, was understood as first & foremost a *revolution of consciousness.* A consciousness, moreover, that necessarily remains *divided.* This division "represents" a fundamental irreconcilability. So that, to begin with, the avantgarde is not any *thing* that can be reconciled under that term: there is no Hegelian movement of sublation or synthesis. For Lacan, the consciousness of not being free at all is the mark of a subjective transference: it is the paradoxical sense in which autonomy expresses itself through subjection.

Let us consider a comparable but inequivalent thesis: that the avantgarde cannot be treated as some *thing* – some artefact or phenomenon or *primitive commodity*[5] – that may be incorporated into an institutional epistemology, even by modifying it – but is rather a kind of *residue in advance,* the inassimilable element of a reduction & attempted sublimation that is *inevitably to come* yet

---

[4] One of the implications here is that – from its every inception – the poetics of the avantgarde has really never been anything more than an elaborate gaslighting exercise on the part of the operations of power (art capital). Just as poetry was the strawman for Plato's ideal (totalitarian) polis. In this hyperparanoiac view, the proverbial "return of the repressed" is a built-in psycho-civilisational diversion tactic, "designed" to maximise the homeostatic operations of power itself. Operations that are themselves paragons of complexity, that only pretend to be those reductive caricatures of "pure reason" by which the world is divided unambiguously between ones & zeroes.

[5] It is important not to lose sight of the fact that – within the history of social crises traced back through the industrial revolution – the universality of alienation & the ubiquity of the commodity form were not *produced* by capitalism, but (by coming to consciousness as the basic teleological condition of value itself) increasingly drove capitalism's evolution towards a general system of abstraction, exchange & (re)circulation.

also *interminable.* In this, the avantgarde is the very mark of the institution as such. In other words, the avant of the avantgarde, & its (neo-) reiteration, is not so much derived from its *coming before* the recuperative act, but its coming into being as the *anticipation* of it: an institutional consciousness before the fact. Here, the supposed "institutionalisation" of the avantgarde resembles the "political" logic of the signifier as expressed in Lacan's seminar on "The Purloined Letter," in which – as Elisabeth Roudinesco summarises – "a letter always arrives at its destination because the *letter* – i.e., the *signifier*, as inscribed in the unconscious – determines, as *fortuna* did for Machiavelli, the subject's fate in its various orientations."[6]

Whatever is experienced as a "true representation" produces an experience of "truth as such"

This "fatalism" of the avantgarde, contrary to Peter Bürger's tragic view, is in no way concerned with institutional escape (the *avant* as line-of-flight), but with a "ruse of reason" (Cixous), by which the institution is constantly lured into an errant terrain ("field") that it can only seek to dominate by valorising the "impossibility" (however symbolic this gesture may be) of doing so. Were we to credit Bürger's assertion that "the art of the twentieth century" can be seen as a movement "to which no historical necessity can be ascribed," then this ruse is all the more remarkable.[7] Its demystifying effect has transformed the work of institutionalisation from totalising omnipotence to hysteric spectacle (whose "content" is anything or nothing). Moreover, this demystification is accomplished on the basis of something which – within the general scheme of power – is afforded a most trivial status. As in the "contest" between Plato's ideal republic & poetry, the dirty work of institutionalisation is always vastly asymmetrical (did poetry ever stand a chance?), yet its elevation as political drama declares that *all is at stake*. To accept that both of these characterisations can be simultaneously true cannot simply be resolved as "capitalist schizophrenia": to begin with, for the reason that the commodity itself isn't an invention of capital but rather the means by which capitalism was able to evolve,

[6] Roudinesco, *Jacques Lacan*, trans. Barbara Hay (New York: Columbia University Press, 1997) 269.
[7] Peter Bürger, "Duchamp 1987," *Avant Garde* 2 (1989): 7.

& to do so in contradiction not only with certain philanthropic views of society, but with itself also – just as the incorporation of "trash" into art, then of "products" & later of "concepts," mirrors those Paracelsian tendencies of a capitalism adrift from fixed value, instead of contradicting them. Rather than signifying the nadir of institutionalisation, the avantgarde here performs a seemingly paradoxical function as its apotheosis – just as in Kant the law comes about & is revealed through *nonlaw*. As Lacan says, "Why is 'liberation' impossible without law?"[8] For this reason, we should be less concerned with the supposed "internal contradictions" of capitalism than with its "revolutions." Likewise, the image of the avantgarde's criminality, its transgressions, its insurrectionary provocations & "revolutionary violence" are not merely a kind of theatre that devolves into repetition, to then be neatly contained within the apparatuses of art capital. If we are to speak of repetition, it is necessary to do so with the full force of its Freudian signification, as the mark of a "primal scene" inscribed within the meaning of the avantgarde & which inaugurates its signifying force at every point. At the same time, this scene operates as a kind of "mirror stage" of subjectivisation – by which the "freedom-to-desire" of the avantgarde is transformed into a "desired servitude" of institutionalisation & *vice versa*.

It is as if Machiavelli's *fortuna* were to elide with Derridean *destinerrance* – such that the institution, via the "detour" of recuperation, doesn't arrive at a higher state of "totality" but instead becomes the itinerary of *an interminable detour*. No matter how "devoid of meaning" the term avantgarde becomes in this process, it nevertheless "determines" the unconscious destiny of its subject, which the institution already is.

This is why Bürger's argument, in his 1980 "Postscript," that "an institution prevents the contents of works that press for radical change in society (i.e., the abolition of alienation) from having any practical effect,"[9] is self-contradictory. In so far as it is meaningful at all to speak of "the contents of works," this content – in relation to the avantgarde – is always already *the institution*. Bürger comes closer to this understanding when he writes, with

[8] Roudinesco, *Lacan*, 346.
[9] Bürger, *Theory of the Avant-Garde*, 95.

regard to Aestheticism,[10] that it represents "that moment in history where the autonomy of the institution comes to manifest itself in the contents of works."[11] The paradigm case for Bürger, which at first appears to represent an extreme point in the negation of Aestheticism, is the Duchampian readymade. In it, Bürger identifies the response to the question Duchamp posed in 1913, "Peut-on faire des œuvres qui ne soient pas 'd'art'?": "At first," Bürger argues, "the readymade seemed to undermine the category of the work of art, now it looks as if even the readymade can be incorporated into it. The institutionalised discourse on art keeps the upper hand over the singular act of negation; but from now on it can make a claim on truth only by integrating its own negation."[12] But rather than supposing the readymade to be Duchamp's reply to his own (rhetorical) question, it needs to be considered that the readymade is rather the "ruse" by which institutionalisation offers itself as the reply, not by integrating its own negation but by affirming its own spectral character (institutionalisation is "revealed" as the mode of production of Benjaminian "aura," whose ritualistic apparatus is equated to that of the commodity fetish).

This relation to auratic spectacle is twofold: in effect, coming in advance of itself, *institutionalisation* is *détournement*.[13]

It is then a question of repositioning Bürger's enunciations e.g., concerning "autonomy" or the "abolition of alienation" (i.e., subjectivity) as issuing from the institution itself in an abstract, metonymic form (unbounded – "like" the Duchampian readymade

[10] To speak of aesthetic autonomy is to necessarily position the question of art & institutionalisation on a continuum with an emergent commodity logic & to recognise the avantgarde as historically coterminous with that logic's critique, not by virtue of chronology but of structure. This relation is the real basis of any "engaged art" that doesn't merely represent a subordination to ideology, but which emerges from the very framework & possibility *of representation itself.* That is to say, of the "autonomy" of the signifier & the arbitrariness of signifying relations (& thus also *of social relations*).

[11] Bürger, *Theory of the Avant-Garde*, 96.

[12] Bürger, "Duchamp 1987," 18.

[13] See Sadie Plant, *The Most Radical Gesture*, 110: "Recuperation & détournement cannot be conceived as the strategies of opposing forces, but the eternal passage between equivalent contexts, so that the revolutionary posters printed in 1968 were no more real or authentic than their 1988 advertisers' simulation; the simulation is not a recuperation, since the original was never outside the play of discursive networks in the first place."

– by any "historical necessity"). Yet it is necessary to go further, to recognise that the institution, *as institution*, thus desires to occupy *both of these positions simultaneously* – as subject & subjectlessness, as aesthetic & anaesthetic, as historical & posthistorical – & it is for this that the (neo)avantgarde functions as a type of imago through which the trajectory of the *institutional movement* is inscribed.

The text isn't a void into which *meaning falls*

Irrespective of the forms it assumes over time, one consistent feature of the avantgarde is its proclaimed incomprehensibility. The naïve view is that avantgarde ""subversion"" of the institutions of (cultural) power derives from the inability of these institutions to *comprehend it*. It's not for nothing that the avantgarde has tended to elide with a critique of rationalism. The subversion of rationalism has always been assumed to be best directed at its modus operandi, its dependency upon categories, coherence, systems. If to *comprehend* is to be held within an ordered system of fixed polarities, then it is easy to see how such a comprehension is anathema to a critique of the *ideology of reason*.

And yet, where this line of argument tends is to the realisation that the institution doesn't in fact need to comprehend anything. If there is any irony in this, it's that the "meaning" of the avantgarde can subsequently be formulated in terms of *precomprehension* or *precognition:* that, *to the contrary*, it functions as an ideological *prosthesis* by which the very idea of the institution *evolves*, & to which it is increasingly bound & dependent upon.

Both the deconstructive force & apparent weakness of this critique rest upon an element of *design* in the avantgarde's pursuit of the arbitrary, the indeterminate, the irrational, as anti-paradigms of systematicity (e.g., Dalí's "paranoiac-critical *method*"). That such design poses avantgardism as first & foremost a *travesty* of institutionalism doesn't diminish its critique to the status of a mock-critique, since this critique begins at a point of self-subversion that in the institution is normally occluded. This *point* hovers constantly on the edge of instability, breakdown, autodestruction: it is the locus of a "desire" that at various times in cultural history has attached itself to terms such as the sublime, transcendence, catastrophe & crisis.

Epistemology doesn't survive its experimental forms

If Bürger recognised in the neoavantgarde a dehistoricised institutional reduplication of what he considered the *historical avantgarde*, it's because he looked within the institution to find it – a gesture of resentment[14] born of "revolutionary disillusionment" (there is a sense, in Bürger's writing, in which the socalled neoavantgarde is *held responsible* for the failure of 1968).[15] The centrality that Bürger's text has assumed in discussions of this "failure" should be reason enough to consider it an act of what Land & others have described as "occult time war."[16] Bürger's critical historiography enacts "powers of incantation & manifestation" *& their opposite*, as weapons beyond mere polemic, to negate an entire field of radical avantgarde activity (including Lettrism, CoBrA, the Situationist International, Gruppo 63, Provos, King Mob, the Motherfuckers, Fluxus, Guerrilla Girls, et al.[17]), in the service of an institutional "hyperstition" that will in effect materialise this fiction & provide the necessary pretence for his rejection of the neoavantgarde.[18] In a classic Situationist reverse, Bürger's self-fulfilling thesis states that every neoavantgarde is a performance of institutional recuperation & that institutionalisation is the precondition of the neoavantgarde. Or, as Lacan said at the time, "the revolution" is never able to free the subject from its servitude.[19]

Likewise in his complaint about all things *neo-*, Andreas Huyssen turns exclusively to the mainstream of postwar commercial art (e.g.,

---

[14] The judgements that Bürger hands down appear to us in retrospect as nothing if not themselves *institutional*. That they are handed down from a position asserted to be from within that of a critical theory, indicates a situation that in itself needs to be more thoroughly examined: of the relationship in Bürger (& elsewhere) between the institutionalisation of the avantgarde & the institutionalisation of theory (the one avowed, the other disavowed: Bürger indeed argues from a position of theoretical high moralism).

[15] As a critique predominantly orientated around the work of Walter Benjamin, Theory of the Avant-Garde appears to take its historical framework & its ambivalences from Benjamin's "The Work of Art in the Age of Technical Reproducibility" (1935). Between Benjamin's essay & Bürger's thesis, the chronology of authenticity's dissolution is simply transposed by several decades.

[16] CCRU (Cybernetic Cultural Research Unit), "Lemurian Time War," *Writings 1997–2003* (Falmouth: Urbanomic, 2018) 33-52.

[17] See, among others, Stewart Home, *Assault on Culture* (1988).

[18] CCRU, "Lemurian Time War," 36.

[19] Reported in Roudinesco, *Lacan*, 343.

"Madison Avenue pop artists"[20]) which he then submits to a flagrantly anti-American critique[21] as if to pre-empt his (& Bürger's) own thesis on the "failure" of this *neo-* as symptom of US culture-industrial appropriation of the aesthetic project of European modernity. Yet none of the many "European" groups operating within this same chronology are brought into the polemic, as exemplifiers of a *viable* neoavantgarde. In Huyssen's *The Great Divide*, Situationism is only referred to as "the Parisian graffiti of May 68" calling for "cultural revolution" & dismissed as a "rhetorical gesture" declaring "the death of all literature" – itself nothing but a recycling of "the traditional anti-aesthetic, anti-elitist & anti-bourgeois strategies of the avantgarde."[22] The events of 1968 are themselves described as having "foundered upon the hard realities of the status quo,"[23] an indictment assumed to be somehow definitive with regard to the Situationists' otherwise "infantile" gesture (Peter Handke's term) – as if Surrealism's encounter with WW2 or Vorticism's encounter with WW1 were not similarly terminal: certainly for Vorticism & Surrealism, yet hardly for avantgardism which, as an idea, immediately spawned Dada & Lettrism, for example, just as the post-68 period spawned Autonomia & Aktionism.[24]

---

[20] Andreas Huyssen, *The Great Divide: Modernism, Mass Culture, Postmodernism* (Bloomington: Indiana University Press, 1986) 168.

[21] Huyssen goes so far as to deny the activities of New York Dada, contemporaneous with those of the Cabaret Voltaire in Zurich. See *The Great Divide*, 167.

[22] Huyssen, *The Great Divide*, 165.

[23] Huyssen, *The Great Divide*, 166.

[24] While tendencies like those of the Italian autonomist movement appeared after the publication of Bürger's text in 1974, the postscript to the 1980 edition makes clear that Bürger saw no reason to modify his text, instead the postscript serves as a response to theoretical & methodological criticisms of the first edition. Nanni Balestrini's 1971 novel *Vogliamo tutto* (We Want Everything) was translated into German in 1972. Significantly, Balestrini's flow chart for an earlier work, *Tape Mark I* (1961), was included in the London Institute of Contemporary Art's 1968 *Cybernetic Serendipity* exhibition & catalogue, one of the first major international shows on the emerging computer art scene – also ignored by Bürger (the very first international exhibition of computer art took place in Brno, Czechoslovakia, earlier the same year, incidentally – curated by the experimental poet Jiří Valoch). A much more credible indicator is Gene Youngblood's Expanded Cinema, which charts many of the pathways in which the technopoetics of the historical avantgarde evolved in the postwar period, often in a Duchampian vein. Bürger's historiography, however, is openly biased against precisely this technological turn in "aesthetics," which – alongside the commodity – represents the major constellation under which a certain notion of autonomy comes to exceed its Romanticist origins.

This entire line of argument appears, in retrospect, determined by an underlying (& unacknowledged) subscription to the premise that avantgardism is bound to the fortunes of capital itself & that only in proximity to the dominant institutions of capital can legitimately avantgarde activity occur: in the postwar situation, this means proximity to a culture industry synonymous with America, whose social organisation is such as to preclude the possibility of any such activity arising in the first place (this is – via Adorno & Horkheimer – Huyssen's unstated thesis).This general argument finds its major institutional moment, ironically enough, in the ascendency of the *October* group of socalled "postmodern" art critics – Rosalind Krauss, Hal Foster, Yve-Alain Bois, Douglas Crimp, et al., which represents a predominantly Duchampian genealogy that runs through Pop Art & Conceptualism, to Fluxus & down to the present. The elisions of Bürger & Huyssen are significant not only in terms of the ideological foreclosure affected by their particular historiographic viewpoint, but for the way in which it bears upon the *October* group's own major canonical revision of western art history, *Art Since 1900* (published in 2014 by Thames & Hudson). Close on the heels of an attempt to manufacture a critical paradigm out of Bataille's notions of the "formless" & "heterology," the *October* group's canonisation of a narrowly-defined avantgardism – as the major impulse in 20th-century art – implies the "forbidden jouissance" of an academicism fixated on resurrecting "transgression" & making a kind of theoretical golem out of it, as – in a perverse refinement of Bürger's critique – the performative agent of an institutional subversion *from within*.

Exceptional conditions are the norm
Yet if we consider the nature of *the unassimilable* contained in Bataille's theory of heterology – which

> opposes every homogenous representation of the world; i.e. every philosophical system... It aims at a complete inversion of the philosophical process that, having formerly been an instrument of annexation, now enters the service of excretion & introduces a call for the violent satisfactions illicit in social existence[25]

[25] Georges Bataille, "Le bas matérialisme et la gnose" (1930), *Oeuvres complètes*

– what we see is that there is, however, no binary opposition: power itself is heterological, there is no truly homogenous philosophical system, & the scientism conjured in Bataille's polemic is a nineteenth-century phantasm at best (contemporaneous as it was with the work of Heisenberg, Poincaré & others). Just as the Foucauldian critique insists that reason *includes* madness, so the abjective functions of excretion are already contained within the "obscene" operations of power. The outward work of exclusion fully corresponds to the otherwise "forbidden jouissance" of excretion in a *fort/da* relation of narcissistic control. There is, in a sense, no "inversion of the philosophical process," since in effect philosophy, as *reason*, is not one system among others (Hegelianism, Phenomenology, Existentialism), but a system-of-systems, just as capital is not one politico-economic system among others but increasingly identifies (through the commodity function) with a logistical capitalisation on emergent structural possibilities (means of valorisation) circumscribed only by dogma.

It is important to grasp, moreover, that between Bataille's notions of heterology & the formless (*defined* as something *like* a spider or spit) & that status of poetry in *The Republic*, a certain equivalence obtains. Not on the basis of abjection or irrationality, but of a dissimulated force. A spider & spit are not, within the western imaginary, significatory voids: the phobia attached to spiders acquires, in Freud's 1932 "Revision of the Theory of Dreams," universal scope in relation to the incest taboo, while in the 20th century spit has potent virological connotations. Likewise, Plato can't truly be said to regard poetry as the language of unreason, on the margin of sense, but as a clear & present threat to philosophy's own claim upon political authority, articulating a realm of thought unforeclosed by dialectics. In each case, the apparatus of subjection constructed in the name of "reason" is little more than an hysterical theatre (in Plato it perversely re-enacts the showtrial of Socrates & anticipates those of Stalinism), whose sole function is to sublimate the insufficiencies of a tenuous, narcissistic "dream of power."

To speak of a "science" of the unassimilable is to speak in precisely these terms – as one might speak of a 'Pataphysics: the

(Paris: Gallimard, 1970) 2:62-63.

"instruments of annexation" attributed to institutionalism appear less connived at, less of an ideological *rationale*, in the manner of a conspiracy against dissent, the free imagination, or merely for the purpose of profit, than they are a kind of "polymorphous perverse" upon which a retrospective rationalisation is imposed in the form of an institutional "ego boundary." (Ideological "science," too, must be subject to contingency & indetermination.) Rimbaud's "JE est un autre" applies nowhere so incisively as it does to the situation of this boundary, to the extent that we might say that this is *all there is*: that if the institution functions as the "content" of the avantgarde, this is for the principal reason that it "itself" *has no content*, it is solely an opening, an orifice, like a blackhole ingesting & excreting in a *purely liminal phenomenon*. That this phenomenon is able to configure the very meaning of spacetime should give us pause for thought as to the gravitational effect of *institutionalisation* upon a cultural field that is often naively characterised as a system of discrete binary relations between autonomous historical subjects.

"To represent" equates to a production of crisis by means of crisis
Contrary to a certain way of thinking about societal & political structures, power does not reign over a state of equilibrium, but exists as a tendency towards states that are far-from-equilibrium. This dynamic, being hierarchical, produces stability from a basis of instability (all dynamic systems are far-from-equilibrium). What is called a *status quo* is in reality a topology of relations-of-maximum-tension, between elements within a system, maintained in a state of perpetual conflict & thus in perpetually evolving balance. This evolution is arbitrary, but the relations it produces are causal, if indeterminate: the system of power is thus neither random nor mechanistic, rather it exhibits the characteristics of what physicists & information theorists call *chaos*. Chaos "reflects predictability over time. A system is said to be stable if it changes very little over a long timescale, & random if its fluctuations are unpredictable. But a chaotic system — one ruled by nonlinear responses to events — may be predictable over short periods but is subject to increasingly dramatic shifts"[26] at larger scales.

[26] Joanna Thompson, "Hidden Chaos Found to Lurk in Ecosystems," *Quanta* (27 July 2022): www.quantamagazine.org/hidden-chaos-found-to-lurk-in-ecosystems-20220727/

It might seem counter-intuitive to say that chaos doesn't represent fluctuations in some predictable, stable norm – but that, insofar as there *is* a norm, chaos is it. And yet this is indeed what observation tells us.

Any far-from-equilibrium system "conceals" dominant chaotic structures within the information that can be used to describe it – i.e., to produce a stable image of what it is & how it operates (over time). For this reason, we must consider, counter-intuitively, a system's "stability" as an expression of its entropy & not the contrary. Likewise, poetic structure doesn't reduce to an inherently "stable" core within an otherwise "chaotic" arrangement of language: any attempt at reduction (Plato's *judicial sublimation* of poetry into the prose of reason) produces only an artefact of its own procedures that *interjects a fictive "sense" into what it cannot comprehend.* (The work of *making (producing) sense* should never be treated as anything other than ideological, while the *preclusion* of its object is not a mark of this procedure's insufficiency but its *(alienating) condition*.) Likewise, the tendency (capacity) to produce such *rationalisations* needs to be considered a measure of that system's *entropy* (& not the contrary). That is to say, of a hermeneutics that works by *deformation* (detour, détournement, etc.). Programmed to assume that all signification must be "stability-dependent," it produces *representations of stability* that substitute for the apparently anarchic operations of poiēsis (& thus mask its own involuted, heterological structures). Moreover, it itself produces the logic of dichotomy on which this appearance is founded. (Power first seeks to totalise *in abstract* (according to the exclusionary principle of binary opposition): it radiates an image of a rectified/ rectifying totality, yet its armature is rather that of a singularity, a blackhole.) The paradox is that, in doing so, it itself "produces" entropy *autopoetically*. (The dialectical image is inverted: the work of totalisation – *as with any system* – always tends *to decoherence*.)

As Lacan argues in his 1971 seminar, XIX ("*...ou pire*"), rationalisation gives way to an "objective persecution" at that point at which a fundamental resistance arises out of a knowledge that appears incomprehensible (what Lacan terms "mathematical incomprehension"). Here we see the dilemma that is already elided in Plato's schema, which has to do with the very status of the poetic object as something knowable – that is to say, subjectifiable – within a schema of philosophical reason – which is to say, of its *power to know*. The dilemma for the Platonic schema thus arises from an *exclusionary force* directed *at what it cannot know*, which it attempts to recuperate by causing to adopt a *rational disguise*. This neurotic double-bind also the mark of institutionalisation.

The longevity of the avantgarde idea, in whatever iteration of neo- or post-,[27] is thus not unlike the Freudian "return of the repressed": in the sense that, being unpresentable within a rigid framework of cultural values, it re-circulates as the trace of its own unassimilability (like Bataille's accursed share). Rather than describing an inevitable trajectory of *institutionalisation*, as convention insists, this re-circulation describes the contrary: the glitch in the teleological scheme whose representation the socalled institution *is*. It isn't a question, therefore, of the inevitable *failure* of the avantgarde project, or whatever it may be called from time to time, but of how it transpires that the omnipotent mechanisms of *institutionalisation* can only represent themselves by means of this apparently minor theatre of dissent, replayed merely (so we are to believe) as a kind of alibi for its on-going commodification under the false appearance of the "new."

The *economic* relation here again invites parallels to the Freudian conception of the unconscious, which Lacan identifies as a circuit: a circuit by means of which the inassimilable thing (the "repressed") is recycled via a network of homeostatic functions within an autonomously "governed" (regulated) system. This "circuit" is in fact an algorithm: a circuit of ramifying feedback loops – in the case of the Freudian unconscious, one of indeterminate complexity which "evolves" over time to behave as if capable of integrating everything. In this it bears uncanny resemblance to Marx's analysis

---

[27] Terms like avant-, neo-, post-, are conventionally employed as if in a time-sensitive relation to the evolution of an ideological system (e.g., western civilisation, the culture industry, etc.), or to the "periodicity" of that evolution, while they themselves are attributed a degree of "chaos" as perturbations on the periphery of a cultural mainstream. By plotting such periodicities against "hidden variables," catastrophic (revolutionary) tendencies of this kind become stabilities. These "hidden variables," like the "hidden hand" of the marketplace, represent the mysterious forces of institutionalisation. What are they? How do they produce magical "transformations," from radically unstable (revolutionary) poetics to artefacts of commodity culture?

of the system of commodities & the illusion constructed by capital*ism*, not merely of being able to "transcend" its own "internal contradictions," but to incorporate any contradiction whatsoever. It is in this respect, but only in appearance, the contrary of the Platonic system of exclusion: in fact, they are identical (the mode of *comprehension* of one is merely a transposition of the other).

There's always a risk, here, of figuring THE INSTITUTION as a malevolent agent of social control, the conspiratorial nemesis of all things "ungovernable." For example, in "Electronic Civil Disobedience," the Critical Art Ensemble state (echoing Foucault, Guattari & Deleuze) that "One essential characteristic that sets late-capitalism apart from other political economic forms is its mode of representing power. What was once a sedentary concrete mass has now become a nomadic electronic flow."[28] In an observation typical of its kind, they note that a new cybernetic mode of understanding information has obscured the location of power, producing decentred structures in which hegemonic relations are distributed across the entire social fabric, problematising the situation of its critique. Consequently, the work of "resistance" needs to be strategically re-conceived. What, however, is lacking here, is a reconceptualisation of the work of *analysing the situation*, a mantra of the revolutionary party that has long since become a mere formalism premised upon the inertia of its critical object.

An important question arises here: if neoliberal forms of "representing power" (that is to say, its "aesthetics") corresponds to a broadly cybernetic conception of autonomous distributed networks, what distinguishes this description from that of e.g. an autonomist "seizure" of the means of production of social meaning? What the Critical Art Ensemble identify as a state of affairs necessitating a strategic reorganisation of the project of resistance, appears in Bürger as a (tragic) situation of revolutionary failure & disempowerment. The termination of the avantgarde in Bürger's schema corresponds here to a termination of the revolutionary project – an "end of history" – & an assent to an *institutional* future (i.e., the failure of the neoavantgarde), impervious to avantgarde strategies of subversion & critique. A curious inversion has occurred

[28] Critical Art Ensemble, *Electronic Civil Disobedience* (New York: Autonomedia, 1996) 7.

here, such that the critical position can now be identified with a "concrete sedentary mass" while institutionalisation assumes the form of an unassailable, polymorphous & ultimately mythological antagonist. Is it not the case that, in doing so, the signifier "institution" is rendered not only ambivalent but attaches to an ideal (because unpresentable) "object" of desire: the mirror of a certain (dissident, avantgarde) revolutionary action itself? In this (illicit) desiring relation, the dyad avantgarde-institutionalisation is reversed, the "failure" of the one transposing into the "success" of the other, not through an incorporation of "ideological content," but in a fundamental restructuring: a restructuring, moreover, that isn't externally affected; it comes about as a general "solicitation" (as Derrida says) of the structure of capital (which is to say, of the system of value) from "within," by way of the operations of the commodity.

Whereas, the institution, in its magic omnipotence, retains all the characteristics of a fetish (a *spectre of power* that haunts the consciousness of every social relation), the commodity names the fundamental *absence* of any such relation, beyond a significatory event that is *without content*. Now the question becomes, to what extent is the "avantgarde" produced (hypostasised) as an effect of this particular hauntology? To what extent does the "avant" correspond to a *preoccupation* with the spectral form of power – a preoccupation that, out of an initial frenetic encounter, acquires the subsequent form of a morbid hypnotic spiral (the *reductio ad infinitum* of two mirrors)? As it is haunted so it is drawn. But drawn to *what*? (There is no ego *in* the mirror.) Is this "institution" not, finally, the mirroring horizon of a perpetual negative dialectics, in which the fatal desire of a certain critico-revolutionary narcissism is put into operation, to come ever closer to this spectre & (as Joyce says) "look upon its deadly work"?[29]

Beja, August 2022

---

[29] Is this, then, the unacknowledged "task" of the avantgarde – to have evolved, by a perpetual economy of institutionalisation, that universal commodity form of which it, itself, is the "tragic" figuration?

90

4. OBJECT SITUATIONS

In June 1933, an essay entitled "The problem of style & psychiatric conception of paranoid forms of experience," by a certain Jacques Lacan, appeared in the inaugural issue of the journal *Minotaure*, alongside a piece by Salvador Dalí that sought to apply the latter's already notorious "paranoiac-critical method" in an interpretation of Millet's *Angelus*. The journal, while not an official Surrealist organ, was edited by André Breton & Pierre Mabille. Dalí's approach contrasted itself to Breton's initially passive definition of Surrealism, as "pure psychic automatism" (per the 1924 manifesto), by proposing an active method of objectification of the paranoiac state, one which presented itself as an uncanny counterpart to the regulation & systematisation of objects of perception (& *their representation*) within a hermeneutics or "discourse of reason." In this, the coincidence of Lacan's & Dalí's texts appears to be anything but coincidental.

By the mid-1930s, Breton, too, was writing about a fundamental crisis of the object, by which the work of psychic automatism was reconceived as *objective chance*. "This still almost unexplored region of objective chance," wrote Breton, "at this juncture is, I believe, the region in which it is most worth our while to carry on our research. It is just on the border of that region in which Dalí has chosen to pursue his paranoiac-critical activity."[1] Where Surrealism

[1] André Breton, "The Surrealist Situation of the Object," *Manifestos of Surrealism*, trans. Richard Seaver & Helen R. Lane (Ann Arbor: University of Michigan Press, 1969) 268.

was first defined by Breton as an "absence" of the faculty of reason, *objective chance* followed Dalí in exploring how the "actual functioning of thought" transcended reason from within & *caused it* to be subject to a certain *surreality*. Like Rimbaud – from whose "poésie objective" the term "hasard objectif" is evidently derived – Breton sought to shift the emphasis of the Surrealist method away from the subjectivism of which it had been accused, towards something *like* an objectivist science. And like Rimbaud, this shift is made to hinge upon a realisation that the relationship between sense & reason is first & foremost one of *formalisation*: that reason isn't innate to its objects but arises out of the way these objects are made to relate.[2] Stated otherwise, at a certain point all descriptive systems of object-relations, such as causality, must be regarded as *ideological*, produced by a regime of valorisation & control. Freud, Einstein, Heisenberg, Bohr & others had already demonstrated this to be the case.

In "The Surrealist Situation of the Object" (1935), Breton writes:

> The practice of psychic automatism in every field came to enlarge considerably the field of the arbitrary close at hand. Now, & this is the capital point, after examining the question, there was a violent tendency to deny that this arbitrariness was really arbitrary. The attention that on every occasion I have, for my part, attempted to call to certain disturbing facts, to certain overwhelming coincidences in works such as *Nadja*, *Les Vases communiquants* & in other later reports, has raised, with an acuteness that is completely new, the problem of objective chance, or in other words that sort of chance that shows man, in a way that is still very mysterious, a necessity that escapes him, even though he experiences it as a *vital necessity*.[3]

Les Vases communiquants is more specific:

> There could be no causal relationship, they tell me. There is no sensible relation between a certain letter that arrives for you from Switzerland & a certain preoccupation you might have had around the time this letter was written. But isn't that making the notion of causality absolute in a regrettable way? Isn't it taking too lightly Engels' words: "Causality cannot be understood except as it is linked

---

[2] See Seth Whidden, *Arthur Rimbaud* (London: Reaktion Books, 2018) 10; 67; 69.
[3] Breton, "The Surrealist Situation of the Object," 268.

with the category of objective chance, a form of the manifestation of necessity"? I will add that the causal relation, however troubling it is here, is real, not only because of its reliance on reciprocal universal *action* but also because of the fact that it is *noticed*.[4]

This "manifestation of necessity," as Breton argues, is both a *real* causal relation & *derealisation* of any causal absolute. Moreover, its reality is both troubling & fixating. Like the Lacanian *objet a*, it inscribes the causal relation as one of an *automation compulsion*, a "vital necessity" that – as both the "cause" & "unattainable object" of its desire – nevertheless escapes the direct experience of the subject, & whose ultimate *unpresentability* (beyond a menagerie of purely "specular·images") thus becomes bound up with a certain aesthetic crisis.

When Rimbaud called for a "dérèglement" of the senses, he wasn't merely advocating a method of psychic *derangement*, but a deconstruction of the *rule* of reason & the *rules* to which the operations of meaning are supposed to conform. Rimbaud's frequently polysemic texts sought, moreover, to decouple signification from a presiding ego: the logos (as in Plato's *Phaedrus*) would no longer be ruled by a paternal dogma. Consequently, rationalism itself would be shown not to be the "father of its logos" but to be a consequence of it. Rimbaud's phrase, "JE est un autre" – from an often-cited letter to Georges Izambart of May 1871 – speaks to a decentring of the Cartesian subject that likewise evokes the ambiguous object-relation of the Lacanian "specular image," or *objet a*, which in turn originates in a reformulation of the Freudian conception of the ego as that "thing that thinks" & which, in thus *representing* the subject's "thought" to it, stands in the place of the

[4] André Breton, *The Communicating Vessels* [1934], trans. Mary Ann Caws & Geoffrey T. Harris (Lincoln: University of Nebraska Press, 1990) 91. Curiously, the attribution to Engels, here, has never been corroborated, nor Breton's claim elsewhere that a genealogy of "objective chance" has Hegelian roots. See Denis Lejeune, *The Radical Use of Chance in 20th-Century Art* (Amsterdam: Rodopi, 2011) 93: "In *Les Vases communicants*, the term 'objective chance' appears in a definition wrongly attributed to Engels: 'La causalité ne peut être comprise qu'en liaison avec la catégorie du hasard objectif, forme de manifestation de la nécessité.' Elsewhere, in his *Entretiens* for instance, Breton traces it back to Hegel. However, Marguerite Bonnet, editress of the complete works of the Surrealist in the three volumes of La Pléiade, interestingly insists in an endnote that she has not been able to locate any such expression in the works of either philosopher."

cause of its desire & of its assumed teleology of action. Lacan draws out the significance of this decentring in his seminar of 1954, in the formulation of a "materialist definition of consciousness," with echoes of Sartre's existentialist phenomenology &, in particular, the scene of Roquentin's pebble-on-the-beach in *La Nausée* (1938).

What is key to all of these considerations of objecthood is the question of autonomy: at *base*, the assumption of an image – not only the "representation of thought," but representation as such – *originates* in the very decentredness *inherent* to mimetic ideology & not in its "violation." Contrary to the kind of assumption that sees Rimbaud & Breton in pursuit of a metaphysics decoupled from the real, we see instead a "return" of the notion of *agency* from the subject *onto the real itself*. Here, it is materiality that *acts* & it does so at the point of an *unpresentability* that in turn is the alienating/alienated condition of representation itself. This is the argument of Bataille's "Base Materialism & Gnosticism" (1930),[5] which initiates a critique of representation from the distinction between materiality & form. Form, for Bataille, is never "objective," but an artefact of valorisation according to a hierarchical-categorical system (rules). Consequently, the "formless" (a spider, or spit) exposes the ideological basis of this purportedly universal "system" (mindful of the fact that even the devalorised & excluded are subsumed by categorisation). In Plato, form, by contrast, is an articulation of truth, which is universally (& objectively) valid, & the entire political philosophy of Platonism stems from this mimēsis. The logic of Descartes – popularised as an expression of the sovereignty of the rational "ego" – mirrors that of the protagonists of the *Dialogues*: the fact of reason mirrors its truth & its truth constitutes the fact of its being.[6]

This circular argument represented the otherwise unassailable foundations of Enlightenment humanism, which both gave rise to & ran aground on the modernist temperament, for which it came increasingly to serve as a grotesque parody. Bataille's frequent (&, by the 1930s, anachronistic) denunciations of "scientific reason" are symptomatic of a wider reaction to rationalist dogma. It's

---

[5] Georges Bataille, "Le bas matérialisme et la gnose," *Documents* (1930) : 1-6.
[6] Lacan: "What is the difference between the imaginary & that which we call symbolism, otherwise called language? ... What the imaginary does is imagine the real – it's a reflection. A reflection captured in the mirror." (Session 4: 9 January 1979)

in this regard that Bataille's conception of the *formless* needs to be understood not as a simple "anti-paradigm" of mimeticism – as in Rosalind Krauss & Yve-Alain Bois' interpretation – but rather as a tentatively deconstructive move within a larger critique of that system of Cartesian rationality by which Platonic thought had become institutionalised as an entire dualistic worldview. A worldview against which modernity in general is the counterargument.[7] If we trace the deconstruction of Platonism & mimetic ideology in Derrida's critique of the mid-6os via the "absolute modernity" of Rimbaud's gesture & its revenance in Dalí, Breton, Sartre, Lacan, Bataille, et al., then it itself comes to assume something like the appearance of a *necessity*, but one that comes in place of any strictly teleological movement. In doing so, it may be said to ruin in advance any attempt to recuperate or institutionalise it – along with the rest of what is referred to as modernity – under the sign of an "incomplete" Enlightenment project.[8]

It's worth, at this point, turning to a more or less contemporary development across the Atlantic, one which takes its momentum from the changed geo-political situation after World War 2. If the war shifted the balance of cultural power away from Europe – in which modernity henceforth equates increasingly to "decadence" – its more "positivist" trajectory in the emergence of a new American aesthetic discourse doesn't necessary contradict (or, as Peter Bürger would have it, *parody*) its historical "avantgardist" condition. The two major antagonists in this narrative are Clement Greenberg & Harold Rosenberg. As defined by Greenberg, the development of modernism was marked by a rejection of mimetic illusionism in order to arrive at "the resistance of medium" – the *flatness* of the picture plane – as a movement toward pure abstraction. For

---

[7] Modernity may be said to name the radical transformation of the understanding of materiality & metaphysics, via the discovery of radiography, TV, x-ray, bacteria, DNA, neuron, etc., & the general abolition of Cartesian dualities. Consequently, the meaning of "materiality" in the context of modernism cannot be reduced to any naïve understanding of the term & tends necessarily to a deconstruction of all "concepts" founded in a system of binary opposition: such as the materiality of writing versus the immateriality of meaning, etc.

[8] The paradox of an avantgarde for which the socalled "project of modernity" is, from the beginning, an "incomplete" conception not because it (modernity) fails in the fulfilment of the task handed down to it from the Enlightenment, but because it is born of a subversion of this very idea.

Greenberg, this movement is nothing if not teleological & the appeal to abstraction bears all the hallmarks of Platonism. Rosenberg, for his part, rejected Greenberg's teleology & considered modernity to be itself a kind of materialisation of historical *discontinuity*.

While Greenberg's theories have come to be seen as cartoonish (not unlike Sartre's), elements of its phenomenology bear further consideration. Principally, while the debate about abstraction has tended to remain entrapped in a trivial dualism with figuration (as two sides of the mimetic paradigm), Greenberg's notion of "resistance of medium" designates not merely a non-representational (or "objective") picture-plane, but the actual circumstance of its *materiality*. In Rosenberg, the same quality of materiality is articulated in terms of *action*. On this point, both resist the otherwise naïve reduction to mere "materials." And while the formal purism of Greenberg's theories are sorely tested in the work of artists like Robert Rauschenberg, the implied *action* of the work's *materiality* points far beyond a simple anti-mimeticism.

Yet if the element of sheer "stuff," or "base materiality," increasingly impinges & demands accounting, this by itself accomplishes little more than valorising in turn those formerly unclassifiable elements of thingness, or even of nothingness – a gesture that could only produce trivial outcomes, of what Bürger calls "shock value." What we come to see, is that it isn't this *inertia* of the "thing" – Greenberg's "resistance of medium" or the "primordiality" of Sartre's pebble-on-the-beach – that produces an existential disturbance significant enough to affect a critique of rationalism from within (as it were) but rather the contrary: it is the capacity of this "thing" to – in a sense – *act*. Or, more precisely, for it to encompass an *action* – as, for example, the commodity in Marx, which ceases to be a "thing" & encompasses an entire semantics of capital; or the unconscious in Freud, which acquires the profoundly ambiguous status of a "thing that thinks."

The force of this apparent decentring, from a *base* materiality to what, in the aftermath of Mallarmé we might call a *signifying* materiality (that is to say, a materiality bound up with signification & not merely subject to its operations), exceeds the temporality of "shock value" in that same way that Pound's invocation of poiēsis as "news that stays news" exceeds mere novelty. The potential to *impinge* thus assumes a materiality & autonomy "of its own," & it is this potential – a potential regarded from the outset as *revolutionary* – that informs the kind of avant-gardist "modernism" whose genealogy runs from Marx, Blanqui & Baudelaire, via Rimbaud, to Breton, Bataille, Lacan & beyond. But in light of the subsequent claims of theorists of postmodernism, concerning the "autonomous" "empty availability" of the aesthetic commodity, it is necessary to consider how these *détournements* of the logic of a certain materiality – as "embodied meaning" & as the "meaning of embodiment" – are not themselves symptoms of a mimeticism whose death has been (as Derrida warns) wildly overstated. Likewise, if a certain materiality of the unpresentable comes to assume the status of an idée fixe within the discourse of modernity itself – whether articulated as a resistance to form/content, or as the tropic movement of signifying possibility in some broader ramification – it remains necessary to ask what, here, is signified under the term "materiality"? And what of "materiality" signifies?

If this is a signal of modernism's incapacity to come to terms with its supposed "object," that is principally because such an incapacity is itself a symptom of a *failed objectification of modernity*. Comparable to anxiety in its psychoanalytic function, the materiality of this signifier *has no object*, yet is itself *in the Real*. And if there remains an insistent demand to question what kind of object modernity *could have in fact been*, this is because, on the contrary, the work of objectification belongs to that ideational mind-eye from which teleology flows forth in single-point perspective. Which is to say: to the imaginary. The persistent tension between abstraction & figuration in modernist discourse, credited to a "crisis in representation," belies the lack of any such teleological situation: a lack which in turn serves as signifier of this *objectlessness*. At which point, to paraphrase Greenberg, the imaginary relation doesn't produce an image, even of itself, but a *medium*. The dyad of modernism/modernity is made to hinge upon it.

One of Lacan's insights was that, like the concept of "value" in Marx, the Cartesian subject is not a unicum (even one derived from a dualistic separation from its object) but a system of (non-)relations: the economimesis identified in *Das Kapital* is always, for Lacan, complexly & dynamically *topological*, a "Borromean knot" in which the Real, Symbolic & Imaginary intersect (if only virtually). Like "fixed capital" in Marx, the Cartesian primacy of the ego is, for Lacan, nothing but an ideological phantasm, produced by a paranoiac desire to objectify possession over reality through self-causation, where instead we encounter an analogue of "objective chance." It is this phantasmatic status that underwrites the evolution of Lacan's work from his article in *Minotaure* to the notorious final ("silent") seminar of 1979, dedicated to the theme of "Topology & Time."

Revealing the onset of a neurological impairment, this final seminar is – in contrast to the great majority of the preceding 30 years, prédominantly visual rather than verbal: when Lacan speaks, for the most part it is to describe the operations of the topological figures he is drawing – with increasing intricacy – on the blackboard. His speech is barely audible. While Elisabeth Roudinesco, in her controversial biography, emphasises the "silence" of this last seminar, what is perhaps more peculiar is that most of the 8 sessions terminate with contradictions:

> As he sank further & further into the infinite "monstration" of the planet Borromeo, Lacan carried out a fantastic work of demolition on the length of the session. For the first time in the history of psychoanalysis, a thinker of genius, with an extraordinary clinical talent, reduced to ashes the great technical principle on which rested the whole edifice of transference built up by Freud. And Lacan did this in order to issue a challenge to science. In the course of a few years, with some of his patients, he transformed the short session into a *nonsession*. This transition to a psychoanalysis reduced to zero went together with the Faustian temptation of the matheme & the knots. Not only did Lacan remain silent & display his knots & braids more & more, but he also lost his power to hear what his analysands were really saying. Instead of listening, in them & in himself, to the reality of what was said, he now tried to hear the basic language of psychosis, like the one Schreber describes in his Memoirs: the language of the matheme, which can reduce to nothing the uncertainty of all ordinary speech. The nonsession was a symptom of this quest: unlike the short session, it didn't allow the patient either to speak-he had no time – or not to speak: he had no time to waste on silence.

At the end of each session, an error in Lacan's description is pointed out by the audience, & in each instance Lacan admits to confusion. The final session concludes simply with the words "Well, goodbye."[9]

In one of the few gnomic statements that Lacan makes during this "monstration," Lacan explains – in the midst of a series of increasingly complex topological diagrams that he spent the sessions drawing on a blackboard – that "The metaphor of the Borromean knot in its simplest state is improper. It's an abuse of metaphor because in reality, there is no thing that supports the imaginary, the symbolic, & the real. What's essential in what I say is that there is no... relation."[10]

Like a character from Ionesco or Beckett, Lacan's descent into riddles, silence & interminable Borromean knots, gives expression to that Freudian *thing* which, speaking from or as the unconscious, is *unrepresentability itself*. The materiality of this "missed encounter," palpable, inscrutable, verging on nothing, at the far edge of language, is like a spectre haunting modernity in the wake of a failed Enlightenment project (the encyclopaedic will-to-represent-*everything*). It is as if the language of the matheme were somehow to *enact* the impossibility of ever getting the world within its grasp, but only through the (mis)understanding of its own impossibility to constitute itself as an ideal ego. What is it, then, that is in fact "speaking" in these final enactments of the Lacanian seminar? What is situated in the lacunae that predominate in this particular performance or non-performance of the "Freudian discovery," which is to say, the Unconscious?[11]

This scene mirrors an earlier scene: a blackboard in a lecture theatre in the Sorbonne on which, during May 1968, someone had written, by way of apparent refutation of *theory*: "Structures don't go out onto the streets." To which Lacan responded: "I don't consider it at all correct to have written that structures don't go out onto the streets, for if there's one thing the events of May prove, it's precisely that they do."[12] And if, as Lacan added, "acts always misunderstand

[9] Elisabeth Roudinesco, *Jacques Lacan*, trans. Barbara Hay (New York: Columbia University Press, 1997) 397.
[10] Jacques Lacan, *Seminar XXVI* (1978-9), session 4 (9 January 1979): apwonline.org/download/seminar-26.pdf
[11] Since it is through the Lacanian "return" that the "Freudian thing" is supposed to speak &, moreover, to speak the "word of Freud" in its apparent objecthood.
[12] Roudinesco, *Lacan*, 341.

themselves," then it is perhaps only by way of an "objective chance" that action advances its cause *in reality*. Objectless action, *sans* teleology: action accomplished in its own transient objecthood. This thing, this objecthood, remains ideology's *other*. It is the locus of a metaphysical "derangement": an "active" materiality affected not by access to some directly lived "authentic" experience, but to an *a priori* "alienation," irreducible either to social pathology or neurotic symptom. Which is to say, to a *mimēsis of the unpresentable*, however "abstract," however "formless," however "revolutionary" it may appear.

Lisbon, December 2022

[ALL THINGS NEW]

...the moment of true poetry brings all the unsettled debts of history back into play...

(Guy Debord, "All the King's Men")

Decolonisation begins right where you are, right where you think
A certain messianic thought in modernity (& its epidemic of *posts*) continues to propel the world towards that perpetual utopia called "the new frontier." But in doing so, its revolution of novelties is accompanied by an utterly reactionary turn. Just as the coloniser washes their hands of the injustices of the Old World Order by inventing previously unheard of injustices in the next one, so a certain species of intellectual forges a path through new & uncharted -isms to evade responsibility for the old ones cast aside. In precisely this way, socalled "leftist moral relativism" points out the trajectory of bad conscience that, like the proverbial finger pointing at the moon, prefers to take aim at collaborators in the social iniquities of exotic & faraway places. It's often said that those who enjoy the privileges afforded by apartheid regimes cannot have remained oblivious to the state of affairs from which their privilege emanates. That a clear line, like a clear conscience, must be drawn between the coloniser & the colonised. Yet the "moral relativist" disclaims *their own* privilege solely to deflect the meaning of collaboration away from themselves, to ventriloquise the colonised & – by asserting the critical equivalence of these positions – to uphold the status quo. In

this scenario, socalled critique profits from the paralysis that ensues from the negation of political struggle by "consensus."

Fortified by the inertia of consensus politics, the status quo projects *itself* as the novel solution to the problem it in fact comprises, just as eugenics forever reinvents itself as the one unifying idea, the communion of the afflicted, the righteous, the vanguard, the architects of utopia. It might readily be assumed that its ideologues know what they are. Have they not, after all, long-dreamt its harsh teleology into being? The great melodramas of injustice & retribution, of extinction & resurrection? This has been the abiding dilemma of revolutionary thought from the outset: the vanguard party that devolves into an apparatus of bureaucratic terror (declared in the name of a "dictatorship of the proletariat" or "democracy" or some other worthy idea) – embodying, in other words, the very spirit of colonialism.

But if modernity failed to deliver on the utopian dream – the dream of reason itself, that *incomplete project of enlightenment* which has left the world even more profoundly in the dark – was this because it wasn't up to the task, or because the task itself was the mark of a delusional thought? Psychiatric wards testify to a superabundance of such rationalised teleologies. Reason, in this scenario, is the doppelgänger of the paranoid schizophrenic. The question is, how did the rationalist technocratic manias of the 19th & 20th centuries so utterly beguile "critical thought" as for it to suppose that a world constructed in their image would be anything other than a madhouse? Or even worse, that the world's repair might simply be a matter of "going back to the drawing board" & refining their formula?

A stone falls from a stony mouth

"They dreamt of... living in a world of pure words... But their private paradise was nothing but the celestial projection of the essence of private ownership. In order to shape it, they had to tear words away from those who could have used them as tools of social... struggle."[1] When the intelligibility of human actions derives from a fictional rationality, language too becomes social fiction. Whereas in every

[1] Jacques Rancière, "The Politics of Literature" (2003).

particular – in the very possibility of its founding relations – society is *actual language*.

The Alienist tract "Poetry & Crime"[2] opens with the observation that "Poetry is suppressed wherever it represents a threat to the rationale of social order." It's easy to imagine that such a statement can only apply to those totalitarian states where "poetry" represents a threat to the prestige of the governing regime, as (under various conditions) it did during the Soviet era. Here "the force of poetry is in direct proportion to its illegality." In the "Free World," the identification of poetry & crime is, by contrast, predominantly an affectation, inherited from modernist Rimbaud outsider-posturing that found its most impactful manifestation in rock music, punk, hiphop, noise. The idea that FBI agents actively infiltrate & subvert "poetry" circles in the US would, taken at face value, appear ludicrous.

Salman Rushdie has been quoted in the media as saying "poetry can't stop bullets," which is very nearly a paraphrase of WH Auden's automatic cliché "poetry makes nothing happen." At best this seems an acquiescence to a state of affairs otherwise self-evident. At worst, a tragic view of the poet as bystander-of-history, with culture, broadly speaking, as its décor. This idea of self-enforced "cultural neutrality," if you like – in place of "aesthetic autonomy" – didn't affect itself by chance. Particularly worth remembering, among the many now documented instances, is that there was a time when Stephen Spender (not coincidentally a close associate of Auden & one-time "US Poet Laureate Consultant in Poetry to the Library of Congress") served as a public relations agent for precisely this kind of dour "pragmatism" – in effect, a useful idiot (however unwittingly) of American "soft power."

There is no avantgarde by consensus
In 1953, during the period of de-Stalinisation, when the intellectual "left" was a more openly contested territory than it had been in the immediate post-War period of Communist Party suzerainty, Spender – along with journalist Irving Kristol (later known as the "godfather of neoconservativism") – founded *Encounter* magazine. In 1958,

[2] Interior Ministry, "Poetry & Crime": alienistmanifesto.wordpress.com/2018/11/04/poetry-crime/

Melvin Lasky replaced Kristol as political editor. During this period & throughout the sixties, *Encounter*'s pages were regularly graced with the work of Eugene Ionesco, Alexander Solzhenitsyn, Arthur Koestler, Ignazio Silone, Malcolm Bradbury, François Bondy, Aldous Huxley & of course WH Auden. In 1967 it was revealed that, via the Congress for Cultural Freedom, the magazine had been funded by the CIA's International Organizations Division (along with MI6). To his credit, Spender resigned upon learning of the CIA's involvement; Lasky remained as editor till the magazine folded in 1991.

The US in particular, via the State Department & its agencies, devoted significant resources to the work of challenging Soviet cultural eminence & countering the idea of Cold War neutralism through such instruments as *Encounter* & the importing of writers like Auden (whose tenure in the US corresponded to his repudiation of previous Marxist viewpoints, accompanied by a reactionary "Anglican" turn). Where the Soviets promoted a poetics openly aligned to the state ideology, the US promoted an "avantgarde" that just as openly proclaimed itself to be apolitical or, as the euphemism goes, "non-ideological." But while US foreign policy may have developed a strategic view of the "cultural front" within its broader Cold War machinations, the idea that poetry – independent of its exploitation by state apparatuses – could have any real, direct bearing upon the "struggle" of Freedom-against-Tyranny was one that could invite only ridicule (while, on the other hand, the blatant jingoism of this "struggle" was expected to be played with a straight face). And yet we must ask how it is that the Cold War – enacted across such varied social terrain – placed such apparent premium upon victory on this "cultural front" in the first place?

Languages of the unspeakable

It's a question that still poses itself today, not only in the context of "hybrid" warfare, but by virtue of the fact that the exigencies of the Cold War did not change with the "fall" of the Soviet Union. The continuing Atomic World Order & its implicit exclusion of direct confrontation between the superpowers, means that even a "hot war" – such as that initiated by Russia's invasion of Ukraine – would necessarily unfold across numerous fronts, including (or especially) the "cultural front," as a proxy for the apparently unthinkable (nuclear Armageddon as automatic corollary of direct military conflict between Russia & the United States). At the same time, a significant amount of agitprop & informational warfare has been directed at the idea that really such a direct conflict already exists, but only on the "cultural front" can this otherwise secret state of affairs be represented, etc.

To properly understand what this question is asking, we need to keep in mind that the birth of Western thought as we know it today – meaning, the birth of metaphysics, which is to say, the *philosophy of the state* (as defined by Plato & represented, in the current conflict, by the likes of Alexandr Dugin & the 19th-century Ukrainophobe propagandist & icon Alexander Pushkin) – was accompanied by an attack upon the idea of poetic autonomy so severe as to demand its *actual negation*, while setting up a species of "official poetry" in its place.

How could this be? How could the cohesion & prosperity of an apparently enlightened, "rational" concept of the state necessitate the reduction of poetry to the status of a political exile made to beg? Let alone the glorification of its parody?

It strikes us as ridiculous that the state & the powers-that-be should be in any way threatened by "poetry," by "poems," or by "poets." Though it is the genius of the state to convince the newly literate masses that poetics amounts merely to this (poetry, poems, poets), rather than the entire discourse of the *possible*. Power is of course concerned with the maintenance of a narrative of *control*; it affects itself as a fait accompli, constituting what is *real*; & what is *real* determines what is *possible*. This is the causal rationale that the state – as the ultimate expression of the doctrine of philosophical reason – is given to represent. But for this representation to carry the authority of the "truth" it apparently conveys, it is impossible for it to admit the contradiction of a poetics; in other words, the discourse of possibility as such, unbounded by the dogma of the state. To understand this in terms of a realpolitik, consider the assassination by cruise missile of Viktoriya Amelina in Kramatorsk by the Russian state apparatus (June 2023) – one in a series of targeted strikes against writers, journalists & arts institutions in whom & in which Pushkinite cultural imperialism is both refuted & exposed as a crime against humanity.

The Nova police...

It's not difficult to see how creating a caricature out of "poetry" – as merely these artefacts (poems) & their alienated producers (poets) – serves an exact ideological end. Power, the state, reason (socalled) has always had an entirely "eugenic" view of poetry: either it must be excluded from the polis & contained in a ghetto, in effect exterminated, or else it may be permitted to re-enter the polis on condition that it collaborate with the ideology of Power (the phenomenon of Elizabethan courtly poetry is very much a case in point, but so too is its apparent antipode, Romanticism, which achieved something of an apotheosis in 20th-century avantgardism: that poetry is also able to exploit & even at times subvert its otheriwse "collaborationist" status, as an "outsider" *within* the polis, is what superficially delineates the latter from the former).

But where poetry had been exiled under the sign of its heresy (unreason, emotionalism, myth), its correlative within the polis acts under the sign of the jester: its truth, its justice, never attaining the status of the "political" as such, even as it serves the unique political function of representing the unpresentable, the impossible, the deadly. Poetry is the fool (Mad Tom), the internal exile, the linguist without a tongue, that turns the impermissible into spectacle & exposes the servility of *all that is permitted.*

Reason in Plato is an *algorithmic* that constantly refines & reduces all discourse to some quality of permission that it calls "truth": that is to say, to ideological agreement [with it]. Plato calls this "dialectic." In it, all discourse is effectively held captive to a supervising, supervening reason; even those it expels are bound to it, since it claims dominion over the *totality* of thought – which is to say, over the thinkable & *the unthinkable.*

Monument men

That Plato demands not only the subjection of poetry to reason but that poetry speak *in the language of reason*, else be rendered mute, perhaps belies an alternative truth: that power (reason) cannot understand it (poetry) – & whether or not it fears what it doesn't understand, what it cannot do is *admit* that it does not understand. When the philosopher-poet Ihor Kozlovskyi was imprisoned for 700 days by the occupying authorities in Donetsk, anything he wrote down was confiscated by the guards during their regular searches. Except for poetry. "They left only poems for some reason. They weren't interested in poetry; they didn't understand them."

Nevertheless, poetry is enchained to the sovereign power it mocks & subverts & is doomed to be buried in the same tomb. The moment poetry is exiled from the ideal polis it is turned, programmatically, into a political vagabond: poetry, by a series of calculated humiliations & assaults, is made to beg for readmission to the state, though not in its own voice but in the language of power (that is to say, in bureaucratic prose, the language of State Reason), & is thereby turned into either a collaborator, a dissident or a political cretin – a "literal" fringe-dweller. This is the default setting of the state: "the awakening of the self," as Adorno & Horkheimer observed, "is paid for by the acknowledgement of power as the principle of all relations."[3] The alternative is to inhabit a non-self, which is to say non-subject, rent through by the "paradox" of a doubly-alienated refusal to submit.

Cast aside by reason for being on the side of "myth" (& the power "myth" exercised over the state *in the place that should have been rightfully occupied by reason*), poetry is doubly excluded as a figure of unreason – & only those "genres" of poetry that are prepared to denounce themselves (in what amounts to an archetypal show trial) might be readmitted – as examples to all who may still doubt reason's power – within the walls of the ideal polis. Yet this casting aside is in fact a political charade, as in the "analogy of the cave" – it performs a work of "gaslighting" poetry into an acquiescence in its own "defeat." (Really, "poetry" is just shadowy figures cast by false light on a cave wall? See, there are the mythic beings to prove it!)

But just as, in Adorno & Horkheimer's reading, "myth turns into Enlightenment," so too poetry is coerced into the work of its own productive transformation. Its act of supplication will take place under a regime of judgement (formalised by Aristotle & cynically designated as a "poetics"), by which poetry is readmitted to the world within a separate domain of "culture" (& cultural knowledge, pedagogy, industry, etc.) in the same way that the "insane" are later admitted into "society" within the institution of the insane

[3] Theodor W. Adorno & Max Horkheimer, *Dialectic of Enlightenment*, trans. John Cummings (London: Verso, 1979) 9.

asylum, under the regime of a political "reason" designed to enforce the internal exile of "mental illnesses". That is to say, within a sociopolitical regime of what Foucault calls "discipline & punishment."

Hieronymo's mad againe

Among such poetries to be subjected to "rehabilitation" not all were assigned the role of inmate or patient – some were assigned that of informant, orderly, capo, amanuensis, whore, commandant's pet. Poetry that refused to thus abase itself was under threat of being cast into oblivion – excluded from the entire mimetic regime of the state, permitted no representation even within the carceral precincts of regulated "culture." Such a poetry (stripped even of its identity) would reside in an underworld of criminality, of illegality – in the same class of political non-being as the terrorist & all other threats to the regime of power that still, somehow, evaded negation, assimilation or psychiatrisation. (It was to this "myth" of a secret poetry of disorder to which the avantgarde would subsequently lay claim – in Debord's words, "The supersession of art is the 'Northwest Passage' of the geography of real life, so often sought for more than a century, a search beginning especially in self-destroying modern poetry.")

What is central to all of this, however, is the fact that the entire dialectical movement of poetry's exclusion & reincorporation into the state can be seen as in no way contingent but rather central to the entire project of reason & its major strategic accomplishment. Thus transformed into an inverse panopticism, the "threat" of any actual dissident poetics was nowhere visible, while its powerlessness was everywhere verifiable. As a "mere" spectre, its very inexistence served a necessary foundational role in the myth of the state born immaculately of reason. Not poetry in any reductive sense, but as general discourse of possibility: the trope-of-tropes, so to speak, of *bringing-to-being.* (Capturing, defining, knowing, authorising "words for Being," as Heidegger would come to say, lies at the heart of the entire metaphysical project.)

Surely reason doth protest too much.

Perhaps to distract from the absence of any real contradiction in the fact that Plato (a dramatist who wrote yet denounced both writing & the seductions of dramatic poetry) should have argued incessantly (in the name of Socrates, the philosopher who did not write, imprisoned & judicially murdered for the crime of "corrupting the city's youth") for the construction of a prisonhouse of reason within which to entrap the conscience of political life, if not life itself...? In other words, to distract from the fact that everything Plato wrote lay in the shadow of a kind of judicial terror, a populist totalitarianism that would sooner murder what it could not understand than examine its own contradictions? (Was Plato's republic therefore a *parody*?)

Proto-Benthamite, by turns hysterical, paranoiac, masochistic: the true character of this dialectical rationale is concealed in plain view, in the very (self-)abnegation of its "method," which is (let us admire the "irony" of it) sheer poetry, a trope-of-tropes. If reason is the method in politics' madness – or merely the palliative for whatever socio-political illness poetry is the symptom of – its inaugurating dialectical movement will have set in course what, throughout the Renaissance, Enlightenment, Industrial Revolution & the Post/Neoliberal present, would appear to be an ideal self-propagating pharmacological regime. A regime via which – like Plato's two-sided pharmakon – both reason & poetry will have ever since been available to the most diverse & contradictory forms of mystification. And while "poetry," not philosophy, would be the "corrupter of youth" for the next 2000 years, it would be reason – evolved under the aegis of the concentration camp, on the one hand, & capital & "capitalist realism" on the other – that would profit on it.

The red plague rid you. For learning me your language!
Such operations of judgement & control – as we see especially in the *Phaedrus* – extend from the most intimate & evanescent moments of love & inspiration to the abstract expanses of "myth" & universal history. But this "inverse pantopticism" mirrors & indeed apes not only the dialectical method but the seeming contradiction between two modes of mimēsis – two apparently contradictory mimetic ideologies (the Platonic & Aristotelian) – which it shows in fact to be *one*: a unified dialectical regime of "representational logic." In other words, of negation & reincorporation: from "truth" as production

of "true representations" (productive of "an experience of true understanding") to "representation" itself availing the "production of understanding" (as "true experience"). It is this regime that not only permits the foundation of a "philosophy of the state" upon a basis of reason, but turns the state into an image of reason itself, which it calls an image of reality: not an image merely of a "political reality" (one among others), but of reality-as-such (with all of the emotive appeal of a fundamental narcissism). And it is in this totalising, narcissistic movement that we see where the danger symptomatic in poetry ultimately lies – in its contradiction of the state's "reflexive" self-evidence & the "singularity" of a "truth" that (while proclaiming itself absolute) requires to be *enforced*.

But what poetry here "represents," above all, is that the reason upon which the philosophy of the state is founded is itself *mythological*. For in expelling those poets in whom the protean forms of myth (polysemy) were an invocation to "actual" history, philosophy – at its paranoiac apogee – sought to construct an image of itself as pure teleology (historical necessity): the state as inevitable political evolution of reason into a monotheism of absolute truth. But if to admit the existence of the heretic it must burn is thereby to admit that the foundations of this "ideal polis" are as purely abstract as it is, the open appearance of this contradiction only fuels an ever-more-elaborately hysterical response – which, "in truth," is what the mimetic regime (of/as power) has always been. A regime as hysterical as it is insufficient. Not the "mass hysteria" of political irrationalism, for which it serves as a doppelganger while presenting itself as an adversary (the hysteria of Socrates' judicial murder being its "primal scene"), but the "pure" symptomatic form of an hysteria that does not arise from, but "is" its very *technē politikē*.

For we should always suspect such an excessive labour of exclusion, negation, recuperation – a labour as susceptible to its own alienating effects as any other labour (but more: a labour that belies alienation *as its own precondition*). We can only wonder that the real power of such a regime to affect the exclusion of "poetry" *in the first place* is as dubious as its self-assertion as political teleology under the rule of reason. Its capacity to orchestrate this entire drama belongs to that genre of utopian writing from which its very philosophy springs – as what, for all intents & purposes, was an act of revenge. It was from the myth of the judicially murdered sage, wise beyond the measure of the state (Socrates, the analogue of Homer, mythical poet & implicit ideologue of the "Greek world" [as Pushkin is of the "Russian world"]), that this revenge derived its righteous indignation. Revenge "against" a system of superstition, corruption, demagoguery & irrationalism (apparently). The work of reason here corresponds to two phases of hysterico-political teleology – corresponding to the Platonic & Aristotelian regimes of mimēsis – the psychotic (paranoiac alienation from knowledge) & the perverse (alienation as paranoiac knowledge). Whereas in psychosis alienation is foreclosed, in perversion alienation is disavowed.

Fiats of unrule

In "poetry," Plato found the ideal subject, by means of which an insurgent "philosophy" could denounce the very powers-that-be it sought to usurp by reasoned argument. More than a scapegoat, the denunciation of "poetry" was a strategic operation, an alibi, a Trojan horse: it permitted, by means of an apparently innocuous vehicle, the infection of the political body & the expropriation of an entire political consciousness. It is the exploitation of a perverse desire, for power to stand, by an "ironic" reversal, in poetry's shoes. Ironic because, to become itself, it was first necessary for philosophy – the discourse of reason – to exit the realm of literature, drama, art, culture in the sense of a collective stupefaction, & acquire a *political language*. A hermeneutics of power arrived at by a derangement (*pace* Rimbaud) of the senses.

If poetry's relation to myth was ever seriously a question for Plato, it was by virtue of this relationship's *precedence.* (Plato's key manoeuvres against writing & poetry are always *by way of myth*, which is simultaneously disavowed – it's an incredible performance.) Poetry's fault was not to be beholden to myth, but its precondition. Its mastery could mean everything. Not because myth could besot the quotidian with the otherworldly, but rather because of myth's *worldliness*, its infusion in all things, the poetics of what Henri Lefebvre would much later call *everyday life*. To stake reason's claim upon political reality it was necessary to cast everyday life as a mode of being constituted through *spectacle* – that is to say illusion, myth, representation, poetics. It was necessary to do this in order to establish a clear separation of the political from the merely contingent & material, & refound it – as the dimension of all social relations – upon abstract principles of reason transcendent (which much later, to the young Marx, would come to bear a disarming likeness to commodity fetishism).

Were it a mere consequence of representation, everyday life – it was supposed – would have no clear consciousness of itself (it could not, according to Socrates' dictum, *know itself* other than through a simulacrum of knowledge: that's to say, poetics). To Plato's mock autocracy – in which everyday life was mustered around an (impossible) principle of enlightenment – Lefebvre & the Situationists responded with a delirious rejuvenation of the "Commune": by which they meant, the *creation of situations* – of a poetic, subversive, audacious "revolution in everyday life." For this, Debord argued, it was necessary to *realise* poetry – which meant "nothing less than simultaneously & inseparably creating events & their languages" both *in place of* & (ironically, parodically) *by means of* the language of power itself (poetry's "revenge").

Poiēsis here *is* revolution: the spectre that forever haunts the state, having preceded it, auguring its end.

That the western media had been perplexed by the fact that 3 stanzas from a Joseph Brodsky poem ("Still Life"), printed in an ornate gold frame, were left by parties unknown on the Russian war criminal & mercenary Yevgeny Prigozhin's grave in St Petersburg, indicates how opaque Plato's lesson remains (how could it be otherwise?). Yet clearly a psychopathology of power still exists in which "the poem," as a kind of fetish or abstract universalism (icon, talisman, trophy, magic charm), "signifies" – but *what* it signifies is made mysterious (like an augury, an oraculation, an incongruous piece of hoodoo).

We don't need to look far, though, to find this pathology in full operation. The Nazi cult was rife with it & its echoes reverberate accordingly through the writings of Martin Heidegger, for whom an occult marriage bound together poetry & metaphysics so as to give birth to *words of power* – or, in Heidegger-speak, *words for being*. We may just as readily say, *words for unbeing:* the fate &

abiding fatalism of "poetry" having marked, ever since Plato (& *as a fundamental precondition*), the way of all incipient Final Solutions – which is to succumb to a lethal self-parody. For power may force history, but poetry unwrites it.

Prague, September 2023

www.ingramcontent.com/pod-product-compliance
Lightning Source LLC
LaVergne TN
LVHW090219180726
843492LV00012B/2101